THE CAT CARE MANUAL

THE CAT CARE MANUAL

BRADLEY VINER

BARRON'S

A Quarto Book

First U.S. edition 1986 by Barron's Educational Series, Inc.
Barron's Educational Series, Inc. has exclusive publication
rights in the English language in the U.S.A., its territories,
and possessions, and Canada.

All inquiries should be addressed to:
Barron's Educational Series, Inc.
113 Crossways Park Drive
Woodbury, New York 11797

International Standard Book No: 0-8120-5765-1

This book was designed and produced by
Quarto Publishing Ltd.
The Old Brewery, 6 Blundell Street,
London N7 9BH

Senior editor Zuza Vrbova
Art editor Hazel Edington
Design assistant Ursula Dawson
Illustrators Craig Austin, Vana Haggarty
Indexer Hilary Bird
Art director Peter Laws
Editorial director Jim Miles

Typeset by Q.V. Typesetting Ltd and
Ampersand Communication Ltd, London
Paste-up by Mick Hill, Penny Dawes, Paul Gardner
Manufactured in Hong Kong by
Regent Publishing Services Ltd.
Printed by Leefung-Asco Printers Ltd, Hong Kong.

• With special thanks to Jane Laing and Lynne Shippam

CONTENTS

INTRODUCTION

The domestic cat is attributed with extraordinarily sensitive organs for hearing, smell and vision that, combined with a highly developed nervous system, make it one of the most finely tuned machines in the animal kingdom.

The domestic cat, known to biologists by its Latin scientific title, *Felis catus*, has been living side by side with humans for at least 4,000 years, although the relationship has not always been as harmonious as it is in the Western World today. Several species of small wild cat are found around the world today that are so closely related to the domestic cat that they will interbreed with feral cats living on the boundaries of human habitation. However, it seems likely that the domestic cat originally developed in the Middle East from the African wild cat, *Felis libyca*, which is larger than most domestic cats but has a lithe body type similar to that found in the skeletons of Egyptian mummified cats. The importance of corn in the economy of Ancient Egypt probably led the Egyptians to encourage wild cats to live beside them to keep down the numbers of mice and rats fattening themselves on their hard-earned harvest. There, from about 1580 BC, an Egyptian cat cult grew up around the goddess Basht, a woman with a feline head who symbolized maternity and fertility.

There is no doubt that the cat played an important part in Ancient Egyptian society as a companion as well as a hunter. The cat certainly played a central role in many religious ceremonies, too. Recent research has shown that almost all the mummified cats were under two years of age — many having been killed by strangulation. Hundreds of thousands of such mummies have been discovered — about nineteen and a half tons were excavated at Beni Hassan in the late nineteenth century and unfortunately sold for use as fertilizer upon arrival in Liverpool. Only a single skull from that vast collection survives.

The domestic cat also figures in early Chinese and Indian literature from around 500 BC — interestingly enough, the myth that a black cat is unlucky can be traced all the way back to Chinese literature of that era.

The cat kept its respected position in Asian societies throughout the Middle Ages up to modern times; it is considered sacred by many of the Eastern religions such as Buddhism. Unfortunately, attitudes in Western society have not always been so sympathetic. While there are many references in Medieval literature and art in appreciation of the cat, particularly in the late eleventh and early twelfth centuries, when Europe was invaded by hordes of black rats that had traveled from the East on boats with the Crusaders, the overriding attitude of European Medieval society to the cat, was one of suspicion and hostility. The Church linked the cat with pagan beliefs. The cat was often incriminated in cases of witchcraft, and indeed it was thought that witches could actually change into cats. In Tudor and Elizabethan England many cats were burned in public as symbols of heresy and agents of the Devil.

Our domestic cat is descended from early climbing carnivores and today, as a species, its closest living relative is the genet (*above*), a carnivore living in the tropical forests of Africa.

Cat artifacts, like this statue decorated with gold earrings (*left*) have been discovered in Egypt and indicate the significance of cats in Ancient Egyptian culture. The goddess Basht, symbolized by the head of a cat with the body of a woman and shown here (*below*) with many smaller cats, was worshipped as a goddess of fertility.

Fortunately, since the late seventeenth century a more enlightened view of the domestic cat has prevailed, with Sir Isaac Newton himself being credited with the invention of the cat flap, or door, for his own pets. The cat's rising status was also assisted by the popularity of the cat with Queen Victoria, who owned two blue Persians. In the United Kingdom, the first National Cat Show was held at the Crystal Palace in 1871, and the National Cat Club was founded in 1887. The cat was first officially imported to the United States in 1749, and the first large American Cat Show was held in New York in 1895.

The changing pattern of Western society has gradually led to an increase in the popularity of the cat and a change in attitudes. While the majority of mixed breed cats used to be kept primarily as cheap and effective rodent control agents, the availability

of modern rodenticides has, to some extent, reduced the importance of that function. However, the cat has become increasingly valued as a companion animal, with its independent lifestyle posing less of a burden than the almost constant attention required by a dog. The cat population in the United States has risen 5.6 percent annually since 1972, while the dog population has held steady or declined slightly, according to a report by Business Trend Analysts. The Pet Food Institute says that in 1985, 50 million pet cats inhabited 25 million homes in the United States and 49 million dogs lived in 33 million households. About 27 percent of all households in the United States now keep cats; 40 percent keep dogs. These figures mark a significant shift from 1983, when 46.3 million cats and 50.2 million dogs were kept as pets.

There is no doubt that companion animals play an important part in reducing the stresses brought on by the impersonal hustle and bustle of modern society. Pets can play an important part in the normal development of children, helping to develop the ability to give and to accept affection, and promoting a sense of responsibility in caring

for their pets. While there are many examples of the beneficial effects of pet animals in assisting the remedial treatment of handicapped children, keeping a pet such as a cat will also help normal children grow into well-adjusted adults.

Although the benefits of cat ownership are enjoyed by humans of all ages, companion animals such as the cat have another especially important role to play in providing company and affection for the elderly, particularly the housebound. It is often impossible for the elderly to give dogs the regular exercise they require, and cats are often therefore more suitable as companions. While the cat may be extremely independent in nature, even the most

Witchcraft has had a long association with cats and this seventeenth century drawing (*left*) shows three witches with their accomplices — a kitten, mouse, owl and dog.

Two feline angels being tempted by Satan himself (*above*).

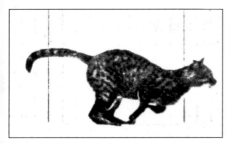

The epitomy of strength, speed and agility, a cat effortlessly makes its way either up or down (*left*).

Body language is important to cats and the arched back (*below*) can either be a sign of aggression or pleasure — the owner will know which.

A cat's gait can be broken down into distinct stages as shown in this sequence (*above*), taken by the Victorian photographer Eadweard Muybridge (1830-1904). The cat's hindlimbs are especially powerful, providing the major thrust for running and enabling the cat to leap on prey.

timid of cats will often relate closely to a single elderly person — most veterinarians are only too well aware of the responsibility of caring for a cat that may be the only close companion for an elderly person living alone. The loss of such a pet will often result in as much grief as would be experienced with the loss of a human partner.

Even in our modern society, with its strident animal welfare lobby, the lot of the cat is not always a happy one. It is all too common for domestic cats to be painfully injured and sometimes fatally wounded by people who find the inflicting of such damage and suffering good sport. There are still cases reported of cats being captured, tortured, and even killed for no reason except sadistic pleasure.

While the ability of an abandoned cat to "go feral" will spare it from the cruelty of extreme neglect commonly inflicted upon dogs, this ability also means that the cat is treated more as a wild animal in a legal sense than its canine counterpart.

The aim of this *Cat Care Manual* is to assist the cat owner with all the information he or she needs to keep this Rolls Royce of "animal machines" in tip top condition, enabling both owners and cats to enjoy many years of happy life together.

SECTION 1
UNDERSTANDING YOUR CAT

THE YOUNG CAT

1

Purchasing a young kitten will bring many years of companionship and enjoyment, but, to avoid any heartache, it is vital to start off on the right path when taking on a new kitten. It is important for you to find a suitable kitten, to settle it in and look after your new pet while it is growing up into a a fully-fledged member of your family. Even the most highly bred of kittens are generally surprisingly tough, so that hopefully, you will be able to deal with many problems that might cause concern in the early days using your common sense.

Exploring the outside world can be frightening for a young kitten.

CHOOSING YOUR KITTEN

The initial and most fundamental choice to be made is between a pedigreed or a crossbred kitten.

? SHOULD I BE GETTING A CAT OR KITTEN AT ALL?

Please ask yourself this question before you make any irreversible decisions about taking on a kitten or an adult cat. It is true to say that cats require less attention than dogs with regard to regular exercise, and an older cat that is going outdoors will not need the same amount of human company as a pet dog. However, there are certain requirements that you must be able to fulfil if you are going to take on the responsibility of a cat:

● Firstly, if you live in an apartment or in some other type of rented accommodation, it is wise to insure that you are permitted to keep pets under the terms of your lease. It is surprising how many people discover that they are not permitted to keep pets in their household after they have gone out and bought their new pet!

● Secondly, unless you are prepared to keep your cat indoors, do you have the facilities to allow your cat outdoors safely? This may be impossible in an apartment, or in a house adjacent to a busy main road without access to a yard.

● Thirdly, although older cats can be allowed to enter and leave the house at will while the owner is out, younger cats and kittens cannot be left at home alone all day. Insure that you can make suitable arrangements if you are out at work — two kittens may be company for each other if they have to be left alone for several hours.

● Fourthly, you must decide whether you can afford to keep a cat. While you may not decide to buy everything listed in the section "What to buy for Your Kitten," there are some costs you cannot avoid:

Food — allow for the cost of a standard can of good quality cat food per day. You may decide to feed fresh food, or supplement the diet with table scraps, but this should serve as a guideline.

Vaccinations — contact your veterinarian to find out how much these will cost. It is a false economy to skimp on these, since, apart from the distress and inconvenience caused if your cat should pick up one of the diseases that can be prevented by vaccination, the costs of treatment would be likely to far outweigh any savings you might make. The cost of regular booster injections must also be considered.

Neutering — again, a telephone call to your veterinarian will establish how much you are likely to need to spend when the time comes. The animal welfare leagues and shelters, various pounds, and American Society for the Prevention of Cruelty to Animals (ASPCA) type organizations may be prepared to assist with the cost of neutering if money is short, especially if you obtained your cat from them in the first place.

Veterinary fees — this can be something of an unknown quantity, depending on the health of

Pedigreed kittens like these Oriental tabbies (*left*) are carefully bred to produce a fairly predictable shape, size and temperament but may be somewhat less hardy than a crossbred kitten, and accustomed to living in the lap of luxury.

A crossbred kitten (*below*) may well be sturdier and easier to look after than a pedigreed one. Regardless of pedigree, you can be sure that your kitten will provide endless hours of enjoyment.

your cat. You should nevertheless be aware that the necessity for treatment may arise, and insure you are able to keep a reserve to deal with it. Veterinary insurance is discussed in Chapter 4, and will help to insure that you are not suddenly faced with a large bill.

Cat litter — surprisingly enough, market research has shown that expenditure on cat litter by the cat-owning public exceeds expenditure on all veterinary services several times over! Include this in your calculations, especially if your cat is to be kept indoors.

Vacations — arrangements for looking after your cat are discussed fully in Chapter 3. Suffice it to say that unless you are able to arrange for someone to look after your cat while you are away, the cost of boarding can add considerably to the cost of your vacation.

• Finally, while it is an excellent idea to take on a cat or a kitten if you have children, do not expect them to shoulder the responsibility for looking after it. By all means encourage your children to play an active part in caring for your cat, but be realistic — the novelty of a new kitten will soon wear off, and

you will probably be left to do a lot of the work yourself, or a lot of supervision, to insure that your pet does not become neglected.

• Remember, a young kitten is hopefully going to be your responsibility for the next sixteen years or more, so think before you decide!

SHOULD I OBTAIN A PEDIGREED CAT OR A MIXED BREED?

More than 90 percent of all pet cats in the United States are not pedigreed. Whereas with a puppy there is always a risk that the small mongrel puppy you purchase will turn out to be a cross between a Great Dane and an Irish Wolfhound, cats are a fairly standard size and shape, and you will therefore have a pretty fair idea of what you are taking on with a non-pedigreed cat. Therefore, unless the characteristics of one breed of cat particularly appeal to you, or you intend to breed from your queen and hope to sell the kittens, go for the crossbreed. Since they are not usually closely inbred, and have a good "mix" of genes, they are likely to be sturdier and easier to look after than a pedigreed cat.

HOW CAN I TELL IF THE KITTEN HAS A GENUINE PEDIGREE?

If you purchase a pedigreed kitten, you should receive a fully completed pedigree certificate showing that the kitten has been registered with the appropriate registration authority such as the Cat Fanciers' Association (CFA) or the American Cat Association (ACA). A transfer certificate to register the change of ownership must be filled in and sent to the appropriate authority once the sale is completed. If at all possible, it is always best to take along to the breeder someone with experience of the breed you are interested in to advise on your selection. You will find that the vast majority of cat breeders are highly reputable, and very anxious to insure that their beloved kittens are going to good homes. However, as in any business, you will find the occasional charlatan out to make a quick buck — so beware!

HOW CAN I TELL THE AGE OF A STRAY CAT?

With difficulty. It may be possible for your veterinarian to make a guess at the age of a cat by its general bodily condition and the state of its teeth, but it is very difficult to judge the age of adult cats accurately in this manner. However, a young cat with deciduous (milk) teeth will be under seven months of age. The permanent canine teeth erupt at around five months, allowing accurate aging at that time.

SHOULD I GET AN ADULT CAT INSTEAD OF A KITTEN?

There are often plenty of homes available for kittens, but giving a home to an adult cat will often save that cat from having to be put to sleep. Since cats are very much creatures of habit, an adult cat will probably take time to settle into a new environment and will probably be fairly set in its ways. There is always a chance that the cat has been re-homed because of ill health or behavioral problems, so a veterinary check-up is a good idea.

CAN I DOMESTICATE A FERAL CAT?

Sometimes. Kittens should be removed from their mother when they are fairly young to be confident of domesticating them — about five weeks is probably the optimum time. Adult cats may be much more difficult or impossible to tame, unless they are used to living close to humans and receiving food from them. These cats normally remain very wary of humans

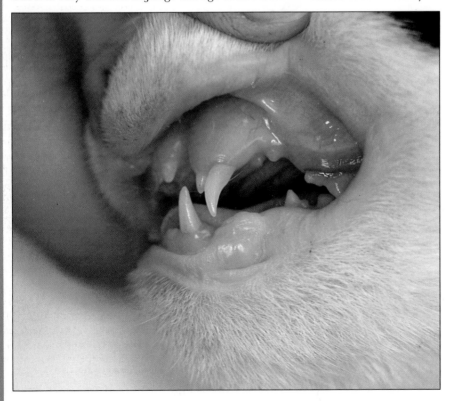

The adult canine "eye" teeth erupt at about five months of age (*left*), which helps in assessing the age of a cat.

SEX DIFFERENTIATION

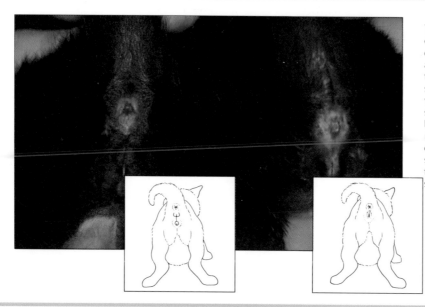

The easiest way to sex a litter of very young kittens is by comparing one sex with another — which is possible if there is an example of each sex in the same litter. The vulva in a female kitten is a small slit-like opening just below the anus (*left*). In the male (*far left*), the small round opening that hides the penis is separated from the anus by the two slightly raised scrotal sacs.

that they are not familiar with, and will probably not be suitable in a household with young children.

? SHOULD I GET A CAT IF I HAVE YOUNG CHILDREN?

Cats and babies generally get on very well together. It is most unlikely that a cat will harm a baby in any way, but to be safe, it does no harm to put a cat net over the crib — cats do love to snuggle up to a warm body if they get a chance. If you already own a cat and are bringing a new baby home, do not ignore the cat or shoo him away. He may come to resent the new baby. Make a big fuss over him and let him get to know the strange animal that has arrived in *his* house, and all will be well.

? WHERE SHOULD I GO TO OBTAIN A KITTEN?

If you want a non-pedigreed cat, it is best to try to find a private home with a litter of kittens that need homes. You are likely to have to pay only a nominal charge for the kitten, and you will have a chance to see the kitten in its home environment with its mother. If you do not know of kittens needing homes through your own contacts, try looking out for advertisements in the local papers, contacting your veterinarian, or any local pounds or shelters. In fact, you may be saving a cat's life if you obtain it from an animal shelter, as shelters always take in far more cats than they are staffed to handle and many may have to be put to sleep if they are not adopted.

It is probably best to avoid buying a kitten from a pet shop if possible. You are likely to have to pay more money for a kitten that has suffered the stress of being taken away from its home and then often brought into contact with kittens from other litters. If only one of the kittens is carrying an infectious disease, it can spread among all those in the shop. This risk of disease will also apply to kittens that have been temporarily housed in an animal shelter, although some of the better ones do have the facility to keep litters of kittens isolated.

If you are looking for a top quality pedigreed cat, perhaps with a view to breeding or showing later on, you should go to a reputable breeder. Your veterinarian or your local chapter of the CFA or ACA should be able to put you in contact with a suitable breeder in the area, or direct you to the secretary of the Breed Association concerned, who is likely to know where litters of kittens are available. Do not be afraid to discuss the matter with your local veterinarian — going to the right place to get your kitten is the first very important step, and it is too late for your veterinarian to offer advice on the matter once you bring your new kitten in for its first check-up.

POPULAR BREEDS

The inherent characteristics, distinguishing features and genetic make-up — from coat color to temperament — of some of the more familiar pedigreed groups.

? WHAT BREED OF PEDIGREED CAT SHOULD I CHOOSE?

If you have decided that you want to purchase a pedigreed cat, then you have a wide range of breeds from which to choose — these are summarized in Chapter 2. The choice of breed is very much a matter of personal preference, although you may already be familiar with a certain breed that you have set your heart on. Since there are so many breeds, and only a small percent of cat owners favor a pedigree, there is little point in devoting a great deal of space to every breed. While it is possible to make broad generalizations about the temperaments of the various breeds, any such generalization is bound to lay itself open to the many exceptions that disprove the rule! The most commonly kept breeds include:

SIAMESE

The most commonly kept pedigreed breed of cat, Siamese are instantly recognizable with their lithe bodies, penetrating blue eyes, wedge-shaped face, and distinctive colored points on the face, ears, and legs. The body should be a pale color, and the points can be any one of a wide range of colors — seal point is the best known, but they can be blue, lilac, chocolate, tabby, tortoise or one of many other variations. Their temperament is equally distinctive, since they are extremely outgoing and demonstrative cats with a very loud and distinctive voice, an energetic and affectionate nature, and a very fierce temper when aroused! They are ideal pets for the owners who want to relate closely to their cat or cats — in many ways their temperament can be more like that of a dog. However, they are

The slim and elegant lines of the Siamese cat are instantly recognizable. The darker colored points on the extremities of the body are classically dark brown — seal, but, selective breeding has produced a whole range of colors including chocolate (*above*) and lilac (*left*).

A Burmese cat (*left*) has an alert wide-eyed look and a more rounded body shape than the angular Siamese. Their coats are sleek and single colored — brown (sable) being recognized as the primary coat color. Other variations have been bred, but in the United States cats with these newer color varieties, such as blue, are known as Malayans rather than Burmese.

The red self-colored Longhair (*below, left*) has an unusual coat color which is difficult to perfect because it should be free of any tabby markings.

Longhair cats have many possible variations of coat color — from the standard blue (*below, lower right*) to patterned coats such as tortoiseshell and white (*below, upper right*).

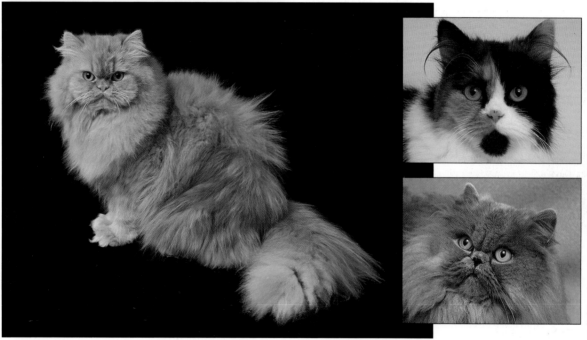

not for those who feel that cats should be seen and not heard! Nowadays, cats with a Siamese body shape and temperament but a solid-color coat, the so-called Oriental Shorthairs, are also available.

BURMESE

The Burmese is another popular short-haired cat with a similar but slightly more stocky oriental-type body than the Siamese and a uniformly colored coat. The primary coat color is brown, but again, a wide variety of colors has been developed. The Cat Fanciers' Association (CFA) however recognizes only the Brown Burmese. They usually make excellent pets, generally playful, extroverted and likely to be less highly strung than Siamese.

LONGHAIRS

Known to most as Persians, Longhairs are distinguished by their long, soft and silky coat, which is most commonly blue, but is bred in a wide variety of colors including white, black, chocolate, lilac, red, and cream, as well as patterned coats such as tabbies and tortoiseshells. Longhairs are renowned for their placid and gentle temperaments, usually making excellent pets and probably able to adapt to a life indoors better than most cats. The long coat makes daily attention from an early age essential, and a Longhair is not for you if you are looking for a cat that will not take up much of your time. However, it is possible to have the cat professionally groomed.

COLORPOINT

Also known as the Himalayan, the Colorpoint is sometimes considered to be a color variety of the Longhair, but it is recognized as a separate breed in the United States. The cat was produced in the 1950s by crosses between Longhairs and Siamese, and should have a Persian-type body with any of the wide range of Siamese colorings. Their temperament is often bolder and more inquisitive than a Longhair, but less so than a Siamese. They are truly beautiful cats when well kept, but require every bit as much attention as any other Longhair.

SHORTHAIRS

These western breeds originated from working non-pedigreed cats of Europe and North America. While these cats may at a first glance appear somewhat similar to a crossbreed cat, over the years the body shape and coat have been developed to a peak of perfection. The European Shorthairs are bred for a stocky, powerful body and head with a dense, rich-colored coat which is found in any of the possible coat colors and patterns, although only a limited number are offically recognized by the governing bodies. They are very tough and sturdy cats, with a calm and affectionate temperament that makes them ideal as family pets.

ABYSSINIANS

Abyssinians are short-haired cats also found with a semi-long coat and called the Somali. They are one of the oldest breeds of cat, always with the classical

American and European Shorthairs are all variations of stocky, short-coated cats, developed from native mixed breeds. The silver spotted tabby British Shorthair (*above*) illustrates the infinite variety in coat-color combinations that have been bred.

Colorpoints or Himalayans have a Siamese coloring with a Longhair coat and conformation, and can be bred to produce the whole range of of colored points found in the Siamese, such as this Blue-Cream Colorpoint (*left*). The intensity of the color at the extremities depends upon a lower skin temperature, so that the long hair of the Colorpoint will tend to result in a paler coloration of the points, but assists in producing the desired pale body color.

The Abyssinian cat (*left*) has a sleek build, but is less elongated in shape than the Siamese. The ears are large and pointed, preferably pricked, with tufts of hair at their tips, emphasizing the alert and athletic nature of this breed.

The Somali has the same ticked coloring and body conformation as the Abyssinian, but the coat is silkier, softer, and much longer. Their coloring is normally ruddy or, more unusually, the rich, brownish, coppery-red, of this Silver Sorrell (red) Somali (*left*).

Russian Blue cats (*left*) have a sleek body shape, with silver tips to the hairs, giving a sparkling sheen to their short blue coat, making it a most attractive breed.

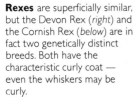

Rexes are superficially similar, but the Devon Rex (*right*) and the Cornish Rex (*below*) are in fact two genetically distinct breeds. Both have the characteristic curly coat — even the whiskers may be curly.

"ticked" agouti coat, although red and blue variations of the usual (golden) color have been bred. Despite their Oriental build, they have a placid nature and are quiet and affectionate pets.

RUSSIAN BLUE

The Russian Blue has a finer, sleeker body than the Shorthair, with a distinctive medium blue, double coat, upstanding with silver tipping to give the cat a beautiful sheen — the coat should not be brushed too flat, or the coloring will be dampened. They are also quiet and affectionate cats that make excellent pets.

KORATS

The Korat is another blue cat, but with an attractive heart-shaped face, large green eyes, and big, tall ears. The coat is glossy and fairly short, with silver tipping on each hair giving the coat an unusual sparkle, although it may take a few years until the coat reaches its full glory. This breed has been known for hundreds of years in its native Thailand, and out-crossing is strictly forbidden. They make very intelligent and loving pets.

REXES

There are two Rex breeds, the Cornish and Devon Rexes — more details of the nature and genetics of their coat types are given in Chapter 2. They are lively and affectionate cats, and although their distinctive coat is not to everyone's liking, they do have the advantage of needing very little grooming. They are exceptional in that they do not shed hair and may be ideal if someone in the household is allergic to cat hair.

SELECTING A KITTEN

Important behavioral traits can be ascertained simply by watching the kittens at play together. The signs of health in a kitten are the same as those in a healthy cat.

The shy and retiring kitten tends to retreat and avoid being handled. It may also be smaller and weaker than its littermates, and in this case, it is called the "runt". It is advisable to resist the temptation to pick this one out of pity, although its weakness may be endearing, because it is likely that it will grow up to be a timid, weak and antisocial cat.

An overly aggressive kitten that scratches its littermates and hisses or snarls unnecessarily when handled gently, will probably not make a good pet, and may well be suffering from an illness.

The bold and playful kitten — lively and eager to come forward and investigate what is going on — is probably more naturally alert than the others. Its forward disposition is a good indication of intelligence and adaptability and so it will make a wonderful pet.

Kittens that grow up together (*below*) will usually become firm friends, playing together and keeping each other company. Although their play-fighting may appear rough, they are not likely to come to any harm.

be simply dealt with by the new owner. In all cases you can look to your veterinarian for advice on the best course of action, and you should inform the breeder of any problems as soon as they arise.

WHAT IS THE BEST AGE FOR A KITTEN TO GO TO ITS NEW HOME?

The usual age for sending kittens on to their new homes is eight weeks, although some breeders may prefer to keep them until they have completed their vaccination course at about twelve weeks. It is possible to move the kittens from five or six weeks of age, especially if two kittens are being homed together. Although kittens sent to new homes at such a young age need more care and attention, they often grow up to become particularly affectionate cats. Older kittens will often settle well into a new home but should have plenty of human contact while still with their mother.

IS IT BETTER TO OBTAIN MORE THAN ONE KITTEN?

Yes. It is delightful to see two kittens entertaining each other, and it is especially important if they are to be left alone a lot. Kittens that grow up together very rarely fail to get on with each other, although male cats must be neutered.

WILL MY PRESENT CAT ACCEPT A NEW KITTEN IN THE HOUSE?

This will depend very much on the temperament of the cat concerned. Surprisingly enough, it is often easier to get a dog to accept a kitten in the house than to persuade a cat to make a new feline friend welcome. However, even if the two cats do not grow to like each other, they will probably learn to live together in relative peace. It is probably best to leave them alone to sort things out between themselves — the presence of the owner often only acts as another source of tension. However, it is wise to keep an eye on them from a distance to insure that no serious fighting takes place.

WHAT CAN I DO IF THE KITTEN I BUY BECOMES UNWELL?

It is always wise to have a new kitten checked over by a veterinarian within a day or so of purchase. If any problems show up at that stage, you will be on much stronger ground when you return to the breeder than if you discover the problem later. The laws pertaining to the purchase of a kitten are in theory exactly the same as for any other goods — they must be of marketable quality and fit for the purpose for which they were sold or you are entitled to your money back. In practice, most owners of a new kitten become emotionally attached to it very quickly and are usually loath to return it to the breeder, even if it is unwell. Unfortunately, it is sometimes better to be hard-hearted and return an unhealthy kitten without delay — nursing a sickly kitten will make you even closer to it and can lead to a great deal of expense, trouble and heartache if the outcome is not favorable. Naturally, many problems that show up in little kittens are very straightforward and can

SHOULD I CHOOSE A MALE OR A FEMALE KITTEN?

Provided that you have them neutered, there is very little difference. However, it is a good idea to bear in mind that, in the future, a cat or a kitten of the opposite sex would be a less threatening companion. An adult cat is more likely to defend its territory more aggressively against another cat of the same sex.

WHAT TO BUY FOR YOUR KITTEN

It is a good idea to have everything ready.

Carrying basket — A plastic-coated wire basket is ideal — the cat can see out so he does not feel trapped, and, unlike wicker baskets, it can easily be immersed in disinfectant if it becomes soiled or if you lend it to a friend. It is much easier to coax an uncooperative cat from a basket that opens from the top than from one that opens at one end. Lay some newspaper inside the basket to soak up any mess the cat might make. Cardboard cat carriers are a cheaper alternative, but are not as strong or long-lasting. Go for the ones made out of plastic-coated cardboard — the plain cardboard ones cannot be cleaned and have a tendency to dissolve if the cat urinates in them!

Grooming implements — It is important to get your cat used to being groomed regularly from an early age, particularly if you have a long-haired cat. Very fine-toothed "flea combs" are not much use against fleas but are excellent for removing dead hair from the coat. Special grooming brushes are available for long-haired cats, and a chamois leather is very useful to finish off the grooming process.

Litter box — This is essential for a kitten or for a cat that stays indoors. The box for a kitten needs to have fairly low sides so that he can climb in — a plastic seed tray is ideal, but adult cats prefer deeper litter and will therefore require a litter box with higher sides. It is possible to buy litter boxes with covers to prevent the cat from spreading litter around the house and to help control odors. A scoop is useful for removing soiled litter.

Litter — Many commercial varieties are available and are readily accepted by most cats. Peat or fresh soil can be used as an alternative, but is likely to be messier.

Toys — Although important for kittens, toys do not need to be elaborate. Just as a child will often disregard the expensive birthday present and play with the box in which it came, a ping-pong ball or an empty thread spool can give hours of fun to a kitten. Toys can also be bought from a pet shop and may be impregnated with catnip to attract some kittens. Do not encourage your kitten to play with yarn — they do find it very attractive, but if swallowed it may cause an obstruction.

Collar — Buy one that has an elastic strip so that it will stretch if the cat should catch its collar on a branch, thereby enabling the cat to slip out of it. A

The new member of the family will feel more at home and secure if it is provided with its own accessories — a litter tray, bed and toys (*left*) — with which it will quickly become familiar.

collar with a name tag attached is of great value if the cat should get lost or become involved in an accident.

Bowls — A china bowl is probably better than a plastic one because it is easy to clean and heavy so that it is unlikely to be tipped over. All bowls and feeding implements should be kept separate from normal household dishes and washed regularly in hot soapy water. Alternatively, disposable foil or waxed cardboard dishes can be used.

Bed — While some cats like to use their own bed, the independent nature of many cats means that they often completely ignore the luxurious basket you have lovingly selected and purchased for them. Fiberglass beds are available, which are easy to clean, and can be purchased with built-in heaters that many cats find attractive. However, a cardboard box with a hole cut in the side will often be equally popular, and can be discarded.

Scratching post — It is a good idea to get your new kitten into the habit of using such a post — rather than your curtains or sofa — from the word go. Several types are available, but one can easily be made by fixing a piece of carpet to a flat piece of wood. The post must then be firmly attached to a wall so that the cat can scratch and pull on it.

LOOKING AFTER YOUR KITTEN

How to make the most of rearing your kitten, and some simple tips on health care and dietary matters.

? HOW SHOULD I FEED MY KITTEN?

Kittens grow very rapidly and therefore require a comparatively large amount of good quality food compared to an adult. At first, it is a good idea to allow a kitten to settle into a new home with as few changes as possible, so obtain a diet sheet from the breeder when you collect your kitten and stick to the same diet for the first few days at least. Once the kitten has settled in, you can gradually change the diet to the type that you prefer — make up your mind how you wish to feed your cat in the long term and get it used to that type of food from an early age. For example, if you expect to feed your kitten on canned food when older, then you should introduce it slowly to one of the brands of complete kitten food available — just as with the adult canned foods, you can be sure that a reputable brand of kitten food will contain all the nutrients your kitten needs. Recommendations as to feeding will be given by the manufacturer on the can. There is no need to feed a vitamin supplement since a complete kitten food will contain them.

By all means feed your kitten on fresh meat or fish if you wish — either regularly, or once or twice a week to add variety to a canned diet. However, it is important that kittens are not fed on fresh meat alone since it is low in calcium and will not provide all the essential nutrients. Be sure that your kitten gets used to a variety of foods, including a small amount of liver to supply vitamin A, a source of fat such as chopped bacon rind, cooked eggs and cheese. Milk is a useful source of calcium, essential for growing bones, but will cause diarrhea in some kittens. A balanced vitamin and mineral supplement is a good idea, especially if your kitten does

A healthy kitten (*above*) should have a healthy appetite. Feed either a balanced commercial kitten food or a freshly prepared diet, but in the latter case, insure that your kitten receives a wide variety of nutrients and does not latch on to only one kind of food.

Drinking milk, contrary to popular belief, is not essential for weaned kittens (*right*), provided they gain their calcium from other sources. Most kittens like to drink a little milk, but some will develop diarrhea if given too much.

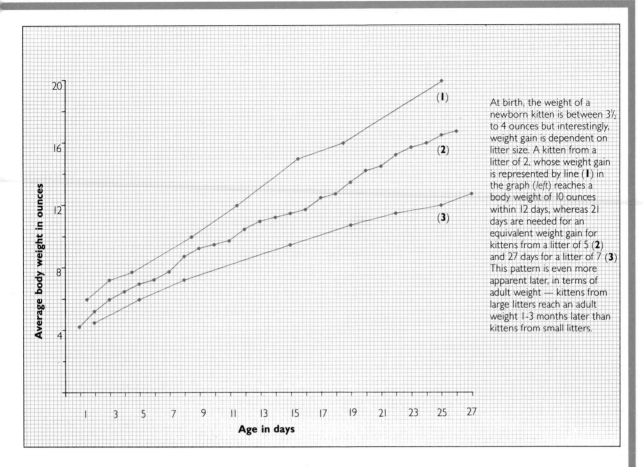

At birth, the weight of a newborn kitten is between 3½ to 4 ounces but interestingly, weight gain is dependent on litter size. A kitten from a litter of 2, whose weight gain is represented by line (**1**) in the graph (*left*) reaches a body weight of 10 ounces within 12 days, whereas 21 days are needed for an equivalent weight gain for kittens from a litter of 5 (**2**) and 27 days for a litter of 7 (**3**) This pattern is even more apparent later, in terms of adult weight — kittens from large litters reach an adult weight 1-3 months later than kittens from small litters.

not do well on milk — your veterinarian will be able to advise you on a suitable supplement for your kitten. Do not overdo the vitamin supplements — while it is important that your kitten receives enough of all the essential vitamins and minerals, it is a mistake to suppose that an extra dose of vitamins will be even more beneficial. On the contrary, too much of certain vitamins can be very harmful. In particular, beware of over-dosing your cat with cod liver oil — it contains large amounts of vitamin A and can cause severe bone deformities.

Obesity is not a common problem in active cats and even less so in kittens that are growing rapidly. Kittens have a relatively small stomach, and it is natural for them to eat little and often — some seem to eat a lot and often! Don't get too worried if your kitten seems to look decidely spherical after a large meal, since even a small stomach can be stretched to an alarming size by a kitten with a healthy appetite. You can generally leave it to your kitten to adjust its intake to its own needs — your kitten will probably waste no time in training you to become the perfect cat owner!

? IS IT NORMAL FOR KITTENS TO HAVE DIARRHEA?

No. The change of environment may cause soft stools for a day or two while the kitten is settling down. If this is the case, take the kitten off canned foods and milk, feeding only freshly cooked white meat or white fish with some cooked rice until the kitten has been passing normal movements for a couple of days. However, contact your veterinarian without delay if:

- The diarrhea is severe or blood-tinged.
- The kitten becomes listless or unwilling to eat.
- The kitten begins to vomit.
- The diarrhea persists for 48 hours.

HANDLING A KITTEN

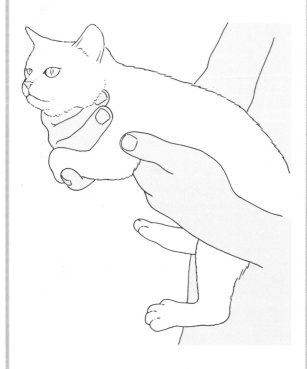

Most kittens will rest placidly if they are securely cupped in the palm of a hand and placed over a shoulder. Kittens love attention and a kitten's personality develops more fully if it is handled and played with. However, you should always be gentle when handling a kitten.

? MY KITTEN DOES NOT APPEAR TO DRINK MUCH — CAN THIS BE HARMFUL?

Cats are very efficient at conserving water and are able to get most of the fluid they need from their food. Some kittens drink more than others. Since urinary problems may be more common in cats that drink very little, try to encourage your cat to drink. You should make sure that a bowl of fresh water is always available even if your kitten does not seem to make much use of it.

? WHAT IS THE CORRECT WAY TO PICK UP A KITTEN?

A placid kitten is small enough to be supported in the palm of the hand. A livelier kitten can be held by the scruff, with its weight supported by a hand under its bottom.

? HOW SHOULD I TOILET TRAIN MY KITTEN?

Cats are fastidiously clean creatures, and training a kitten to use a litter box is not usually too difficult. Watch the behavior of your kitten, and you

will soon be able to read its mind! You will notice that it will start to sniff around for a suitable place. This is the time to pick up the kitten and gently deposit it in the litter box — the kitten will soon start to scrabble around to dig a suitable hole. Offer your kitten plenty of praise and affection when it has performed in the box, and it will soon rush there, eager to please its new owner.

? HOW OFTEN SHOULD I CHANGE THE CAT LITTER?

It is important to keep the litter box clean, or cats will refuse to use it. Feces should be scooped out as soon as they are found. If the box becomes so dirty that you have to do more than just dump out the litter and rinse it, then you're probably not cleaning it out frequently enough.

? WHAT SHOULD I USE IN THE LITTER BOX?

Many brands of commercial litter are available, and are hygienic and generally contain some sort of deodorizer. Most contain fullers earth, but some are made from compacted wood shavings.

A litter tray should be available to your kitten at all times (*left*) and the cat litter should be changed regularly. While a deep litter tray is best for adult cats, the sides of the tray must obviously not be too high to prevent a kitten climbing into it. Fortunately, cats are naturally clean creatures, and toilet training comes naturally to most kittens.

Exploring the big wide world for the first time is an exciting experience for a kitten (*right*). Most cats will not venture out into new territories until they have found their bearings and are capable of returning home. However, it is best to only allow kittens out into a securely fenced garden so that they are unable to escape until they are older — and hopefully wiser!

Some kittens seem to prefer alternative types of litter — peat or fresh soil can be used. While the latter is somewhat messy, it does seem particularly attractive to many cats and might be useful for cats that are unwilling to use the litter box.

? WHEN AND HOW SHOULD I START LETTING MY KITTEN OUT?

Your kitten should not be allowed to come into contact with other cats until the vaccination program has been completed — usually this will be at around 13 or 14 weeks of age, but ask your veterinarian for advice relating to the vaccine he or she uses.

? HOW CAN I GET MY KITTEN OUT OF THE HABIT OF USING A LITTER BOX?

Having spent the early part of your kitten's life encouraging him to use a litter box, you may well decide that you would like to dispense with it when your kitten starts going outside. Most cats will prefer to eliminate outdoors once they go out regularly, but you should not be surprised if at first they come running indoors to use the box! It is probably best to keep the litter box available for a "rainy day" when a cat may not want to go outdoors. It might start eliminating around the house if a box is not available.

? HOW CAN I STOP OTHER CATS ENTERING MY HOUSE VIA A CAT FLAP?

Cat flaps are very useful, since they give cats a degree of independence to come and go as they please. However, you might find that you have a problem with unwanted feline friends entering via the flap. It is possible to purchase cat flaps that are activated by a magnetic collar on your cat and will therefore not allow any other cats to enter. Or you can lie in wait for an unwanted intruder, armed with a water pistol. A spraying with water will not harm a cat, but will probably convey the message that it is not welcome!

CAT FLAPS

Ideally, both the cat and the owner should have some kind of independence from each other and the easiest way of attaining this is by installing a special cat door. It should be fitted snugly near the base of an ordinary exterior door or wall, at a comfortable level for the cat to simply step through. A cat will need some initial help or basic training in learning to use the flap efficiently and there are several kinds of flap available. The most popular design (1), has a light spring or magnet which automatically closes the door after exit or entry and so prevents drafts. A simpler contraption (2), only swings outwards and the cat must either be let in and out or taught how to lift it with its paw. Alternatively, the cat can use a simple opening (3), fitted with flexible plastic triangles.

Cats groom every part of their body thoroughly (*left*) and spend a considerable amount of time doing so. They lick their paws and use them to groom any areas that their tongue cannot reach.

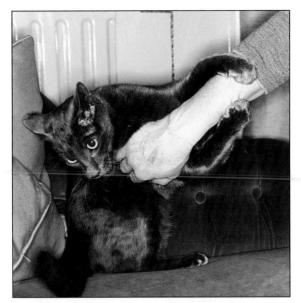

Play-biting, wrestling and rough-and-tumble games, either with a human companion (*above*) or with littermates are typical play traits in kittens more than four weeks of age — all part of learning to be a cat.

The surface of a cat's tongue (*below*) is covered in fine spikes, which act as a natural comb to groom the coat and remove any debris.

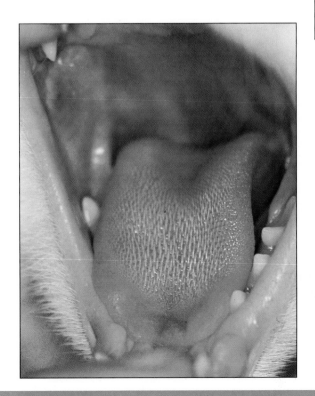

? IS IT CRUEL TO KEEP A CAT INDOORS?

It is obviously natural for cats to roam freely outdoors, although some timid cats will show no desire to explore the big wide world. If you keep a kitten indoors from the time that you obtain it, it will come to accept that its territory only extends as far as the front door. This may be the only way to keep a cat safely if you live next to a busy main road.

? IS IT IMPORTANT TO PLAY WITH MY KITTEN?

Yes, particularly if you have only one kitten rather than a pair. Playing is a natural part of the learning process of kittens and should be encouraged.

? HOW CAN I STOP MY KITTEN FROM BITING AND SCRATCHING ME?

If your kitten has an aggressive personality, it may get rather carried away when you play and start to attack you with teeth and unsheathed claws. Although this may seem cute and harmless in a young kitten, it should be firmly discouraged. Stop playing with the kitten immediately and ignore it. When it has calmed down, start playing with it again very gently, speaking with a soft voice.

? WHY DO CATS GROOM THEMSELVES?

Grooming has several important functions in the cat:

• Removing dead hair and cleaning the coat.

• Stimulating the skin glands to produce their natural oil secretions and spreading them over the coat to waterproof it.

• Keeping down the number of skin parasites such as fleas.

• Eliminating mats that can cause a skin infection.

• Vitamin D is produced by the action of sunlight on the skin — this is then ingested during the grooming process.

• Cooling down in warm weather — cats do not sweat through their skin but utilize the evaporation of saliva from their skin to cool themselves down in warm weather. This is why grooming tends to be more common in warm weather or after strenuous activity.

• Enjoyment. Grooming is an important social activity in groups of cats and is presumably an enjoyable pastime. When stressed, cats will often be seen to groom themselves as a displacement activity. This is rather like someone repeatedly adjusting and re-adjusting his tie nervously before an important interview.

GROOMING EQUIPMENT

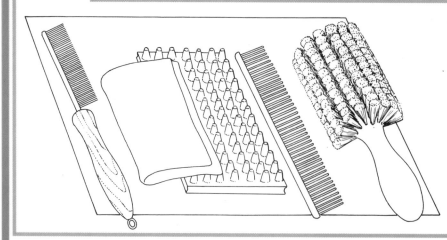

The most important implement for grooming a kitten is a fine-toothed metal comb (*far left*). For a particularly tangled coat, though, you may find it easier to remove the bigger knots using the coarser-toothed comb first. A brush will assist in removing dead hair, but is not as effective at removing any knots and debris. Stroking the cat with a chamois leather cloth will give the coat an extra shine.

? DO ALL CATS NEED REGULAR GROOMING?

Many short-haired cats will be able to look after their coats perfectly well on their own — you can encourage your cat to groom himself by smearing a little butter on his coat. However, grooming is very important for long-haired cats such as Persians, and even some short-haired cats seem to need regular assistance. It is very important to get long-haired kittens used to being groomed from the outset — don't wait until the coat is severely matted and grooming becomes painful for the kitten. If your kitten resents grooming, do a little at a time very gently until it becomes used to it.

? SHOULD I BATHE MY KITTEN?

While there are some cat owners who have got their cats used to being bathed from an early age, bathing your kitten is not necessary or advisable except in exceptional circumstances such as severe soiling of the coat with oil or tar (see First Aid section). Regular grooming is far more beneficial and less traumatic.

? CAN KITTENS BECOME ACCUSTOMED TO WALKING ON A LEAD?

Take an adult cat and put it on a lead and it will sit and look at you as if you have gone insane! However, if you accustom your kitten to exercising in this manner when it first begins to go outdoors, many will come to accept it as the natural thing to do. Some breeds such as the Siamese seem to take better to this than others, and you might consider it

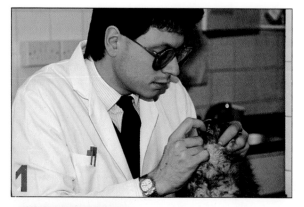

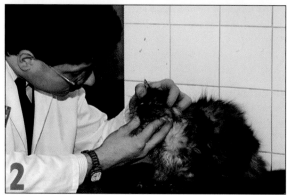

1 The mouth is a good indication of the cat's overall health (*above, top*). The gums should ideally be pink and the teeth white, although those of an older cat may be slightly yellowed.

2 The eyes should be free of any discharge or redness (*above*) which may be an early sign of cat 'flu.

GROOMING A LONG-HAIRED KITTEN

Regular grooming is vital for long-haired cats, and you should accustom them to being groomed from an early age. Using a wide-toothed metal comb, groom the legs free of any tangles, then comb the belly, flanks, back, chest, neck and tail — all in an upward direction, fluffing up the hairs. Then, brush the coat, also against the lie of the fur and complete the routine by rubbing the cat with a chamois leather.

3 The ears are examined (*above, top*) for any infection or excessive wax which is indicative of ear mites.

4 The coat should be free of mats with no trace of fleas or other parasites (*above*). Check for skin sores or any bare patches — a sign of ringworm.

as an alternative to keeping your cat indoors if you live in an inner city area. In a similar manner, most cats will become very nervous when transported in the car, but some who have become accustomed to it from an early age will travel quite happily this way.

? SHOULD I CLIP MY CAT'S NAILS?

Preferably not. Most cats will keep their claws in good shape by scratching and climbing outdoors, or with the use of a scratching post indoors. If you feel it essential to clip the nails because of the damage your kitten is inflicting upon you or your furniture, then remove only the very end of the nails with special nail clippers — if you cut them too short you may catch the quick or cause the nail to splinter.

? WHEN WILL MY KITTEN LOSE ITS BABY TEETH?

The permanent teeth will begin to push through at about five months of age, and your kitten should have all its adult teeth at about seven and a half months. While this process may pass almost unnoticed by the owners of some kittens, other kittens can be caused considerable discomfort by this change of dentition. It helps to know that the incisors come through first, followed by the appearance of the first molars and then the canine teeth. The adult cat has a total of 30 teeth.

• Despite any experience you may have had with teething babies, never give a cat aspirin or similar painkillers.

HEALTH CARE FOR KITTENS

Preventative medicine is an easy option to ward off common ailments that kittens are susceptible to.

? WHAT DISEASES SHOULD MY KITTEN BE VACCINATED AGAINST?

Vaccines are at present available against feline distemper or infectious enteritis (otherwise known as *panleukopenia* and respiratory disease. The latter disease can be caused by several different agents, but the vaccines protect against the two most important viruses involved. These diseases are discussed in more detail in Chapter 4. If your kitten should catch these viruses, there are no drugs that can be used to kill them. Your veterinarian will only be able to treat the symptoms while your kitten tries to fight them off. Prevention really is better than cure with these diseases, so be sure your kitten is fully protected before allowing him outdoors. The exact timing of the injections will depend upon the particular vaccine used, but they are most commonly given at nine and twelve weeks of age.

? WHY DO SOME KITTENS "WOOLSUCK" AND CAN IT BE HARMFUL?

Just as with babies, sucking seems to offer comfort to many kittens even after they have been weaned. Some kittens will get into the habit of sucking on material, particularly wool. This should not be encouraged, because the kitten will swallow the fibers which can cause a bowel obstruction. If possible, remove the material that is being sucked.

Vaccinations should be given to a kitten when it is about two months old — before then some immunity is acquired from the mother (*above*).

Sucking wool is common in kittens but seems to be an inherited habit as it is more prevalent in pedigreed breeds. Although it may be a psychological comfort to a kitten, it should be discouraged (*left*).

It has been suggested that kittens are more likely to woolsuck when they are hungry, or if they do not have enough fiber in their diet. You could try experimenting with a change of diet to see if that helps — sometimes ad lib feeding with dry cat food seems to stop the problem, but is not advisable as the sole long-term diet. Extra fiber can be given in the form of wheat bran, available from a health food store, mixed well into the meat or canned food.

? ARE THE VACCINATIONS NECCESSARY IF THE KITTEN IS NOT GOING TO COME INTO CONTACT WITH OTHER CATS?

If you can be certain that your kitten will never come into contact with other cats, then it is most unlikely that it will contract any infectious disease, although the virus that causes feline distemper is very resistant, and it is theoretically possible that it could be carried into the house indirectly on clothing or shoes. However, if your kitten grows up in a very sheltered environment and then suddenly comes into contact with disease when older — for example, if it escaped from the house — it would have very little natural resistance to infection. It would probably become very ill indeed — much more so than a cat that was going outdoors all the time and boosting its natural resistance. The kitten would, of course, have to be vaccinated if you wish to board it. Modern vaccinations are very safe, and it is wise to have your kitten protected even if you do not expect to allow it outdoors.

TRANSMISSION OF A VIRUS

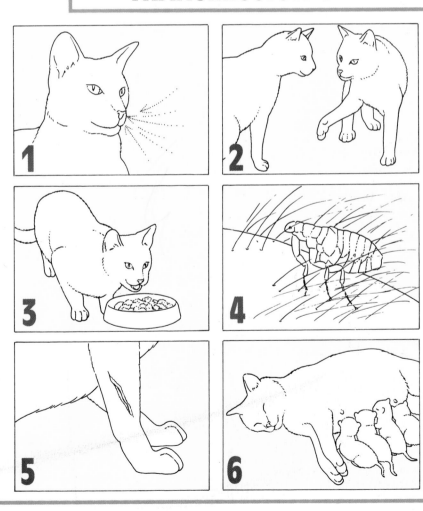

There are several ways that a virus may spread from cat to cat. It may be airborne (**1**), in droplets that are coughed or sneezed, as in the transmission of cat 'flu. Some of the more resistant viruses such as Feline Panleukopenia may simply be transmitted on contact (**2**) or indirectly on contaminated items such as bedding, grooming implements and feeding bowls. Feline Panleukopenia is also an example of a virus that is transmitted by being ingested in food and swallowed (**3**). Other kinds are spread by bites from insects or other animals (**4**). Open cuts and wounds are another way of transmitting a virus (**5**). A particular danger to developing kittens is that some viruses are small enough to pass across the placenta, or contaminate the mother's milk and infect newborn kittens (**6**).

? HOW CAN I TELL IF MY CAT HAS FLEAS?

You may find an actual flea (although they are difficult to spot), or it may find you! However, fleas are on the cat for only a small proportion of their life cycle, so even if you do not find any on the cat, it still may be infested. If you comb the cat with a fine comb you may well find "flea dirt", which is the flea's droppings and contains mostly dried blood. This dirt can be distinguished from grit that may have got into the coat by putting it on a damp cotton ball — since the dirt is mainly dried blood, it will give off a reddish-brown "halo".

? HOW CAN I GET RID OF FLEAS?

Because fleas lay their eggs around the house, any treatment should involve the environment as well as all animals in the house. Any bedding that the cat uses should be burned, or at least thoroughly washed, and insecticide should be used around the house. Use a preparation specifically designed to kill fleas on the ground. This is different from the cat spray.

There are several ways of treating the cat itself for fleas: shampoos are of no use for long-term control; flea collars are better than nothing but are not usually 100 percent effective and may cause a localized skin reaction; powders are sometimes the only application that a cat will tolerate. The most effective means of treatment is regular spraying with an insecticide. Your veterinarian can supply you with drugs that are stronger than you can buy at a pet shop. Fleas seem to be resistant to many of the less potent drugs. The best way to hold a cat for spraying is for one person to restrain the cat while another sprays the cat against the lie of the hair.

? ARE FLEAS MORE COMMON AT CERTAIN TIMES OF THE YEAR?

Yes. The life cycle of the flea slows down or stops completely when the temperature drops, and when it warms up again the fleas emerge from their cocoons. Consequently fleas tend to be more of a problem in warm weather than cold, although they do thrive all year around in warmer climates or in centrally heated houses, and often cause a particular problem when the heating is first switched on in the fall.

Fleas will usually cause a cat to either scratch or groom itself excessively (*above*). You may not be able to find the actual fleas, but you may well be able to see the "flea dirt" — reddish brown comma-shaped flea droppings.

DEFLEAING

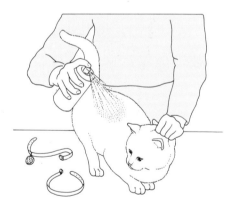

Regular treatment of both the cat and its environment is essential to remove all fleas. To treat a cat with a spray or powder, grasp the cat firmly by the scruff with one hand, and spray or powder into the lie of the coat with the other hand.

This task is easier and more effective if performed by two people — one to restrain the cat and the other to administer the treatment. Always read the instructions on the product before use.

LIFE CYCLE OF A FLEA

1 Adult cat fleas (*right*) are about one-twelfth of an inch in length and flattened from side to side. They feed by sucking the blood from their victim, and then jump off in order to lay eggs in the environment. One flea may lay up to 500 eggs in its lifetime.

2 Their eggs (*below*) are laid on the cat's bedding, or anywhere else that the cat lies. These then develop for between two and sixteen days, depending on the external temperature and humidity, and then hatch into larvae.

4 The larva normally develops within the cocoon (*above*) for about two weeks before emerging as an adult flea. The cocoons are very resistant to insecticides and disinfectants, and since they hatch in response to vibrations, may remain dormant for months, or even years.

3 The larvae (*left*) are about one-eighth of an inch long and actively burrow down into bedding, carpets or upholstery, away from light. They feed on household dust and debris, and may also pick up tapeworm eggs. After about a week the larva forms a cocoon.

KITTENS AND ROUNDWORM

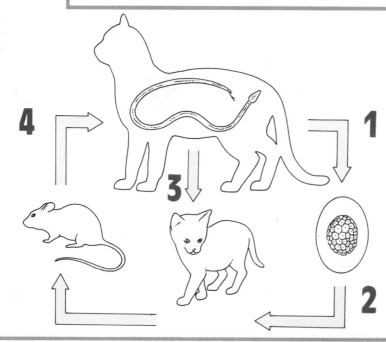

Ascarid roundworms grow in the intestines of a cat (**1**) and feed on the digested food there. Their eggs (**2**) are passed on via feces, which may be swallowed by another cat and if this happens, the larvae hatch in its intestines. The danger to a newborn kitten is that the larval stage of the *Toxocara cati* species migrate to the mother's milk at the onset of lactation and infect the kitten (**3**). Alternatively, the eggs of either of the known species of roundworm, *Toxocara cati* or *Toxocascaris leonina*, in the feces may be eaten by another animal — such as a beetle, bird, rat or mouse (**4**) — that a cat may prey upon and so in turn infect the cat.

? HOW DO I KNOW IF MY KITTEN HAS WORMS?

The most common worms found in kittens are roundworms — the adult worms are long and thin like lengths of string. Occasionally a kitten will vomit adult worms or pass them in the stool. The eggs are shed in the stool, but they are so small that they are not visible to the naked eye; your kitten may well have roundworms without your knowing. Since roundworms can cause such problems as a pot belly, tummy upsets, or even intestinal obstruction, it is wise to treat all kittens regularly against roundworms. Your veterinarian or a pet shop will be able to supply you with a suitable drug.

Your kitten may also pick up tapeworms — the adult worms are long and flattened, but small segments like grains of rice are passed in the stool and will probably be noticed either in the stool or stuck to the hair around the kitten's anus. Tapeworms cannot be passed directly from cat to cat. They must be carried within the body of an intermediate host, which, in the case of a kitten, is most likely to be a flea. Tapeworms are somewhat more resistant to treatment than roundworms and the most effective drugs can be obtained only from your veterinarian. It is also important to carry out regular flea treatment to prevent reinfection.

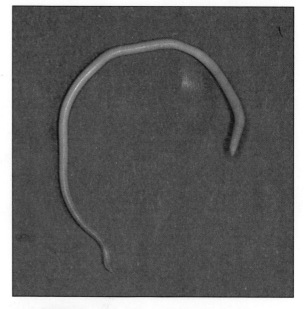

Roundworms are white, long and round, growing to a length of up to four inches. Common symptoms in a kitten are a weakness, a dull, dry coat, a pot belly and sickness and diarrhea which may contain visible worms — a help in diagnosis. Kittens infected at birth can be treated when they are two or three weeks old.

❓ WHY DOES MY KITTEN HAVE BLACK WAX IN HIS EARS?

Ear mites — eight-legged animals about half the size of a pinhead — are commonly found in the ear canal of kittens and older cats. Sometimes they do not seem to create any problem, but more frequently they cause irritation of the ears and the production of large amounts of dry black wax. They are fairly easily treated with anti-mite drops (known as *acaricides*), but since the drops will kill off only the adult mites and not their eggs, treatment must be continued for three to four weeks to prevent recurrence.

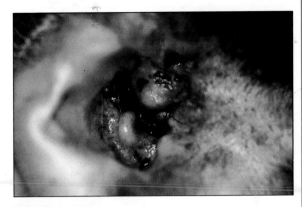

Dark brown ear wax (*above*) is a symptom of ear mange, due to mites, which is relatively prevalent in the cat world and so can easily be passed on to a kitten.

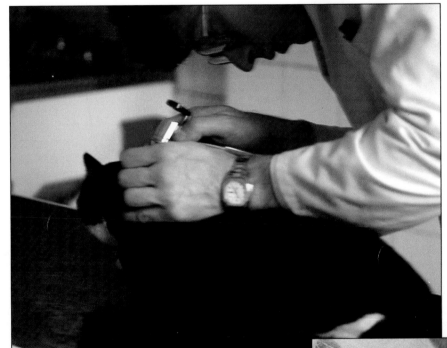

An auriscopic examination, using an illuminated magnifier (*above*) to see inside the lower part of the cat's ear, enables the veterinarian to identify the basic cause of an ear problem (see p.123).

The cause of an ear disorder needs to be diagnosed as soon as possible as persistent scratching around the ear can lead to self-injury and the formation of a skin hematoma (*right*) or blood blister, which in turn will also need veterinary treatment.

THE ADULT CAT

2

To maintain a good, fulfilling and stable relationship with your healthy, adult cat, basic health care and delicate every day issues such as feeding, neutering and traveling need to be appreciated.

The principles of genetics are vital for anyone intending to breed from their queen, fascinating in terms of predicting particular characteristics that your cat may have inherited and intrinsic to explaining popular questions such as "Are tortoiseshell cats always female?"

Having a queen rear a litter of kittens is a wonderful experience and advice on pregnancy, the birth and the rearing of young kittens is invaluable.

Alert, stealthy and playful
— antics of an adult cat (*right*) that are really a relic of the hunting tendency.

FEEDING

Cats are like miniature lions in that they are carnivores. Their nutritional requirements in terms of sustenance and essential vitamins and minerals, can only be derived from meat, fish and animal fats such as milk.

? IS IT BETTER TO COOK FRESH FOOD RATHER THAN FEED PREPARED FOODS?

There is nothing wrong with feeding your cat with a balanced diet of freshly prepared foods, but it is not essential. The manufacturers of the reputable brands of commercial cat foods put a lot of work into insuring that they contain a balance of all the essential nutrients your cat needs. By far the largest proportion of cat food sales in the United States are of dried foods, with approximately 90 per cent of

cat owners feeding it at least once a week. Surprisingly, the most popular brand is also one of the most expensive. You may be able to fool your dog into frugal eating habits, but cats are notoriously selective as to what they will and will not eat — very often only the best will suffice! Cats also seek more variety in their diets than dogs and will become bored with the same diet day after day. However, most are content with a regular change of the flavor of canned food offered. If you are one of the many owners who get pleasure from carefully preparing fresh food for your cat, then you may rest assured that you can feed your cat a perfectly healthy diet by taking care to provide a reasonably wide variety of food, including some animal protein and fat and a reputable vitamin and mineral supplement. Next time you take your cat to your veterinarian for a health check or routine vaccinations, take the opportunity to discuss any dietary matters you might be unsure about.

? IS IT HEALTHY TO FEED DRY CAT FOODS?

Dry cat foods are convenient and hygienic to feed; they help to exercise the teeth and are ideal to put out if you have to leave the cat alone in the house for a period. Unlike so many of their owners, most cats are pretty good at regulating their food intake and avoiding middle-age spread. However, dry cat food seems to be highly popular with many

A fat cat (*right*) is not necessarily a contented one. Although most cats seem to be able to eat just enough food to maintain a normal body weight, weight control in cats can be a problem in those few cats that do not regulate their own intake sensibly, particularly if they are able to find food elsewhere — it is not uncommon for one cat to be fed at two homes. Attempting to fill up the cat's stomach with high fiber foods may be an answer, but your cat may not agree!

cats and can easily overcome their natural weight control mechanisms, leading to obesity. In addition, many cats do not seem to drink enough extra water to make up for what they are not getting in the food, causing them to produce very concentrated urine. This may lead to urinary problems, especially in neutered male cats. Dry foods are fine as an occasional treat, but they should be avoided if your cat has had a past history of urinary problems, such as cystitis, or is so enthusiastic that it tends to become "hooked" on them and refuses to eat other foods.

❓ HOW OFTEN SHOULD I FEED MY CAT?

Since cats are generally good at regulating their weight, it is usually all right to feed a little and often on request. Your cat will quickly have you trained to respond to his or her demands for food! Be sure the bowl is always cleaned out before food is put into it — most cats will only eat food that is fresh and wholesome and will object to the smell of stale food.

❓ WHAT CAN I DO IF MY CAT IS OVERWEIGHT?

Often not a lot. If your cat is an indoor cat and you are prepared to withstand persistent demands for food, it is relatively easy to simply feed smaller amounts of the normal diet. Unfortunately, most owners have little control over their cat's food intake, since it will seek food elsewhere if not enough is provided at home. Keep away from the more fattening items such as dry cat foods and milk and try to fill the cat's stomach with bulking agents such as bran. Playing with your cat will help to increase the speed with which food is burned up — most self-respecting felines look with disdain upon their canine counterparts who allow themselves to be exercised on a leash!

❓ WHAT SHOULD I GIVE MY CAT TO DRINK?

Always be sure that fresh water is available for your cat, but don't be surprised if it chooses to drink elsewhere. Many perfectly normal cats drink very little, getting the fluids they need from their food. Other cats prefer to drink outdoors, or from less conventional sources, such as a running tap, hot bath water, or even from the toilet. Our simple human palates seem inadequate to appreciate the subtle differences in flavor that are so important to our feline friends!

Canned food does contain carefully balanced amounts of protein, fat, carbohydrate, fiber and mineral and vitamin supplements that mimic a cat's natural prey. If your cat only eats dried food, insure that it drinks plenty of water as well.

SHOULD I OFFER MILK?

It is not essential for cats to drink milk, but some cats are very fond of it. Too much milk may cause diarrhea and encourage obesity, so do not allow your cat to drink to excess. Of course, milk can turn sour very quickly, so be sure that it is not left out too long.

ARE THERE ANY FOODS WHICH CAN BE HARMFUL TO CATS?

As is often the case, too much of a good thing can cause problems. In particular, an excess of liver in the diet can result in severe bone disease due to the large amounts of vitamin A it contains. And a diet of canned fish only can cause *pansteatitis* or "yellow fat disease", a painful inflammation of the fatty tissues due to vitamin E deficiency. Raw fish contains an enzyme that breaks down vitamin B1 and can lead to a deficiency. In general it is best to cook fresh foods and remove any bones.

WHY DOES MY CAT EAT GRASS?

We're not sure of the reason, but it seems to be quite a common habit. It might be an attempt to take in extra roughage or an attempt to clear the stomach of hairballs. Or perhaps cats simply like the taste! In any case, it is a good idea to offer housebound cats some grass in a pot and to discourage them from chewing houseplants, which can be poisonous.

WHY DO MANY CATS LIKE TO EAT CATNIP?

Nepeta mussinii, otherwise known as catnip or catmint, is very popular in the feline world. It contains a chemical called nepetalactone which seems to have a similar effect to that which a large gin and tonic would have on their owners, releasing their inhibitions and making them more playful than normal. Some toys are also impregnated with this chemical. While the effects seem to be pleasant in most cats, some cats seem to react aggressively, sometimes to the extent of attacking their owners. This reaction is very uncommon, but it would be worth removing anything containing catnip if aggression is a problem.

Milk and cream are appealing to most cats (*above*) but some are unable to digest it very well, and may develop diarrhea if they drink too much.

Meat or meat-derived products form the staple diet of most cats as they are generally fairly conservative in terms of taste. However, some cats do have more adventurous palates (*right*), and will eat vegetables or starchy foods and this kind of variety should be encouraged.

Chewing grass is a popular pastime with many healthy cats (*left*) although, sometimes it may be a sign of an impending digestive upset. Housebound cats should be offered pots of grass.

A healthy appetite is often a sign of a healthy cat (*below*) although, some cats are prone to fads. Watch out for any change in your cat's habits, since it may give a warning of an impending problem.

? CAN MY CAT BE VEGETARIAN?

It is not advisable since they are *obligate carnivores*. In other words they have to eat meat in the wild while some other carnivores, such as dogs, can manage in the wild on a mixed diet if meat is in short supply. Cats have lost the ability to make certain essential amino acids not found in protein of vegetable origin. A deficiency of the amino acid, taurine, can cause progressive blindness. Cats also require a much higher fat content in their diet than most other animals and vegetarian diets tend to be low in fat. In the wild, their diet would be composed of small rodents, frogs, toads, birds and insects; so be sure that at least a third of the diet is protein of animal origin. Vegetarianism is fine for humans and all right for dogs, but cats need meat!

? CAN I FEED MY CAT DOG FOOD?

No. While it will not do any harm to give cat food to a dog, dog food will probably not contain all the essential nutrients your cat needs. Additionally, some of the dog foods contain preservatives which are poisonous to cats.

? SHOULD I WORRY IF MY CAT DOES NOT EAT FOR A DAY OR TWO?

You will quickly become familiar with your cat's habits — some cats will go without food for a couple of days for no apparent reason, whereas others are absolutely regular in their eating habits and will alert you quickly if something is amiss. Remember, however, that in the warmer months particularly your cat's predatory instincts will come to the fore, and he may get food elsewhere. Even if your cat is too lazy to pose a threat to the local wildlife, a friendly neighbor may be offering food. If your cat is otherwise well, do not worry if he is off his food for a couple of days. Should your cat seem at all unwell, or not eat for more than 48 hours, it's time for a visit to your veterinarian.

FELINE BODY LANGUAGE

Cats may not be able to speak to us, but they are equipped with many means of communication.

Cats are sensual creatures, and their body language is highly developed. Most feline signals have been developed for communication between cats, both within a group, as a means of reinforcing their mutual bond, and between rival cats, to mark the limitations of their territories, and to attempt to keep intruders at bay.

Like us, cats have their own intrinsic individual personalities. But, there are also other traits, with an ancestral root, that are common to all cats, that have specific meanings which can easily be translated. For example, cat's claws, when unsheathed may be used as a dangerous weapon but they are also used as a means of communication — to scratch "marker posts" for delineating territory. On the whole, in real terms, domestic cats play-fight with their owners and other cats with their claws sheathed.

Cats also have other responses that are not quite so easy to interpret because they have a physiological basis. For instance, a cat will sometimes stretch its neck, open its mouth and curl back its upper lip in a sort of a snarl — an automatic nervous response, the *Fleshman Reaction*. It enables the cat to draw chemicals onto the tongue and then up onto a special area above the roof of the mouth, called the Jacobson's Organ, which connects directly with the area of the brain concerned with appetite and sexual behavior. This kind of reaction is particularly common in tom cats seeking out a calling queen.

Grooming in cats is not just a matter of personal hygiene — it reveals the highly idiosyncratic nature of individual cats. Cats groom themselves in response to fright or indecision — a typical displacement activity.

Feline "vocabulary" includes growls, hisses, screeches, purrs and just plain meows — a wide variety of sounds used mainly to communicate with other cats (*above*) but sometimes, also with owners. Siamese cats are particularly vocal, and will often have "conversations" with their owners.

Licking is a very important form of communication between cats, beginning with the attention that a queen will give to her kittens, (*left*), but carrying on into adult life between cats when they are relaxed together.

The pupil of a cat's eye will dilate widely in response to anger, fear, aggression and sexual excitement (*far right, bottom*). A long, slow, blink from a cat is a sign of relaxed contentment, and may be used as a greeting (*right*). The markings around the face often accentuate the eyes (*far right, top*) — a natural eyeliner!

Cats' ears are erect if alert (*above*) but pulled down flat if angry or scared (*right*). Hearing in cats is far more acute than ours, and the trumpet-shaped ear flaps can be used to direct as much sound as possible into the ear.

The tail is an obvious indicator of the mood of your cat. It is held high when happy and alert (*above*), twitches at the end when mildly irritated and is bushy and fully erect when spoiling for a fight.

Cats' paws are used to knead against a favorite spot when very contented (*below*). This is a throw-back from kitten behavior, when the suckling kittens knead against their mother's breasts to stimulate her flow of milk.

TALKING CATS

Cats actually possess a "language" that consists of three basic sounds — murmurs, vowels and strained high-intensity and high pitched shrieks. Murmuring includes purring and other soft sounds that are made with the mouth shut, used for greetings, calling for attention, acknowledgment and approval. Purring is a sound associated with extreme contentment and it is remarkable in its continuity — cats can purr for hours with hardly a change in rhythm or intensity. Although we know that cats can vocalize when breathing in as well as when breathing out, biologists are not exactly sure how cats make their purring sound.

The cat forms distinct words by closing its mouth to terminate each sound and most cats have a small "vocabulary" of essential sounds that may mean "in" or "out" or "feed me". The different way cats pronounce their vowel sounds gives them their individuality and distinctive recognizable voice. Similarly, human voices can be distinguished and differentiated in this way.

High-intensity strained sounds are generally reserved for inter-cat communication. To vocalize these, the cat's mouth is kept open and tensed and changes shape. A growl may be emitted in anger or

Sacs that secrete a very strong scent, are located on either side of the anus, may be emptied when the cat is frightened (*above*).

The hair will stand erect when the cat is angry or frightened. Combined with an arching of the back, this has the effect of making the cat seem as large as possible in an attempt to scare off any intruder (*left*).

Whiskers (*right*) are very sensitive to touch and are used to establish an initial contact with a friend. Touching of whiskers is followed by rubbing bodies along each other.

a piercing shriek when in pain. Many cat owners may also be familiar with the curious tooth-rattling stutter of frustration, produced when an inaccessible bird is seen through a window.

FIGHTING CATS

Making faces is another fundamental mode of feline communication. A happy cat has perky ears and relaxed whiskers whereas an angry cat keeps its ears erect but furled back, its pupils constricted to slits and its whiskers "bristle" forwards. A frightened cat is wide-eyed and lays its ears and whiskers flat. Most of these expressions are exhibited during a confrontation between two cats.

Flighting between animals of the same species, usually occurs either over a suitable mate or to protect territories. It has a ritualized form, with plenty of hissing and snarling.

The hair in a cat is unconsciously controlled by the autonomic nervous system and if the cat is angry or frightened, the hormone adrenaline is activated, making its hair fully erect so that each animal appears as large as possible. As often as not, the smaller or weaker cat gives up its challenge before a major fight breaks out, and usually only minor scratches and bites are incurred.

Sense of smell is very important for territory marking (*above*). Special scent glands are present on the skin below the ears, on the foot pads, and on the base of the tail — when a cat affectionately rubs its head and body against you, it is actually marking you with its scent.

BALANCE AND MOVEMENT

Some aspects of the amazing agility and grace — due to specialized sense systems — exhibited by our feline friends.

The cat's nervous system is perfectly adapted to interpret the wide range of information received from the highly developed sense organs, and to coordinate the movements of the finely tuned muscles, bones and sinews that make up the locomotory system. The modern cat is still very much a hunter at heart, with a strong muscular fast-moving hunter's body, and is usually able to return to the wild and fend for itself if necessary.

Cats are unique animals in that they can move in so many different ways — from sinuous stretching, stealthy and almost unnoticeable creeping to rapid powerfully controlled leaps and jumps. The flexible skeleton and superbly supple muscles give cats their twisting and turning ability, and enables them to squeeze through the smallest of gaps.

Cats have a sophisticated internal sense of body orientation which is apparent and familiar to anyone who has watched a cat move. It is achieved by a combination of supersensitive sense organs. Cat's eyes are exceedingly acute which, combined with a balance and orientation monitor — the vestibular apparatus in the inner ear — enable the cat to respond instantaneously. In effect, a cat can correct itself with a reflex response.

Probably the most well known feline attribute, in terms of movement, is the righting reflex — the ability to land on all fours from a fall. An automatic sequence of movements, that are completed within the split second of a fall, enable a cat to land safely without harming itself.

Firstly the cat always adjusts its head to an upright position and the body follows by rotating and twisting accordingly, prior to landing. Any other subtle readjustments to balance, on landing, are perfected by the tail.

Curiosity may supposedly have "killed the cat", but ladders are for climbing and the world is for exploring (*above*). Cats are natural climbers, often feeling less vulnerable to attack from less agile creatures when off the ground. Coming down may be more difficult than going up, but most cats will manage it, if left to their own devices.

Yoga-like stretching movements (*right*) seem to come naturally to cats — humans need years of practice to achieve similar feats.

Cats love maneuvering small objects (*left*), or prey, using their sensitive paw pads and the enormous flexibility of their forelimbs — achieved by the lack of a collar bone.

Walking on a fence is a circus trick for us, but an everyday experience for cats, who are able to stroll along calmly (*above*).

An ordinary position for a cat (*right*) but, try this position for yourself and see just how supple the feline body is!

The streamlined body shape of a cat enables it to "fly" through the air with the greatest of ease and combined with superb coordination, to pounce on prey (*above*).

SEXUAL BEHAVIOR

Rarely observed, but often heard, copulation actually stimulates the release of eggs from the ovaries of the queen. Sexuality is the key to many of cats' behavioral traits.

? WHEN DO CATS BECOME SEXUALLY MATURE?

This will vary depending on the breed of cat and the time of the year — Oriental breeds tend to mature earlier than most, and Longhairs tend to mature later, but on average, female cats start to call at about seven months of age while tom cats produce sperm a month or two later. Female cats that mature in the winter months may not start to call until the spring — though the presence of tom cats and other calling females may encourage a female cat to start calling. There is a classical veterinary joke about an elderly spinster who brings a young female cat with a swollen tummy to the veterinarian and says, "She couldn't possibly be pregnant — I don't let her out, and the only other cat in the house is her brother". Beware — cats are not quite as selective in their choice of partner as we might like to think!

? HOW CAN I TELL IF MY QUEEN IS CALLING?

Again, there can be a great variation between breeds, with Siamese queens calling so loudly that the whole street knows about it and Longhair queens so quiet that their owners are hardly aware that they are on heat. The queen may go off her food and become restless, sometimes rolling around the floor as if in pain and often sitting at the window and howling to get out if kept confined. The "call" of a queen in heat may come as quite a shock to inexperienced owners; they often telephone their veterinarian in a panic thinking their cat is unwell. You can tell the difference by grasping your queen by the neck and stroking her along her back by the base of her tail; she will react with great pleasure if in season, treading with her hind feet, lifting her rump, and pulling her tail to one side. Even if your queen calls fairly quietly, the

A roused tom approaching a female from behind, as she rolls provocatively and treads with her front paws.

The tom grabs her by the scruff of the neck and, arching his back, mounts her, front legs first. The female twitches her tail aside.

local toms will soon hear of it, and the presence of an eager crowd on your doorstep should alert you to the fact that she is in demand!

? HOW CAN I STOP MY QUEEN FROM CALLING REPEATEDLY?

If you do not wish to breed from her, then spaying is the obvious answer. However, if you do wish to breed at a later date, it is possible for your veterinarian to give drugs to stop her calling for a while — these drugs may be in the form of tablets or an injection. Female cats are *reflex ovulators* — they do not produce an egg to be fertilized until the act of mating has occurred. It is possible to induce a "false pregnancy" to stop her from calling by stimulating the vagina with a cotton wool swab to mimic mating — breeders may keep a vasectomized male cat for the same purpose. However, it is not recommended that this method is used repeatedly because it may produce an abnormality of the womb.

? AT WHAT AGE CAN A FEMALE CAT BECOME PREGNANT?

It is perfectly possible for a kitten to become pregnant the first time she calls — usually at around seven months of age. There have been reports of Oriental-type kittens calling when they were only three months old, but some cats, particularly Longhairs, may not call until 18 months of age. Female cats do not have a menopause, and will usually continue to be able to have kittens until they are about 14 years old — there have even been reports of 20-year-old cats becoming pregnant!

Both male and female cats are usually very promiscuous in their breeding habits. Although a maiden queen may resist mating at first, she is soon likely to become receptive to the advances of several tom cats, each mating repeatedly.

• A receptive queen will crouch down and lift her rear in the presence of a tom cat, pulling the tail to one side and making treading movements with her hind legs.

• The act of mating in the cat is a quick and violent affair. The tom cat grasps hold of the queen's neck firmly with his teeth while treading with his hindlegs. Penetration and ejaculation occur in a matter of seconds thereafter.

• Immediately after mating, the female cat will call out loudly and turn to attack the male, who, if he has any sense, is by then beating a hasty retreat. The queen will then roll around on the ground and lick at her vulva region.

This process will generally be repeated after several minutes, with most male and female cats mating together about seven times.

Afterward, the queen pulls forward, crying out and turns on the male who makes a hasty retreat and then washes.

The female also washes, voluptuously, and after some minutes, she may well pat the male and they begin all over again.

? AT WHAT AGE SHOULD I ALLOW MY QUEEN TO HAVE HER FIRST LITTER OF KITTENS?

Many kittens become pregnant either by accident or design in their first season, and problems are uncommon. However, many breeders would prefer to wait until the female cat is a little more mature, and mate her on her second or third season when she is likely to be about a year old. A queen should not be allowed to have her first litter after she is four or five years old.

? HOW CAN I FIND A SUITABLE MATE FOR MY QUEEN?

In the case of a non-pedigreed cat that is going outdoors, it is usually a case of "Don't call us — we'll call you". Tom cats will usually appear from nowhere, eager to offer their services to a queen in heat. However, if your female cat has a pedigree and you are aiming for a classier match than your local tom, the first step is to find a suitable stud tom for her. This is best done through the Breed Society for your particular breed of cat — usually the Secretary will be pleased to offer advice and may well have a list of stud toms for your breed. The address of your Breed Society is available from the governing bodies — the Cat Fanciers' Association (CFA), the largest cat registry in the United States

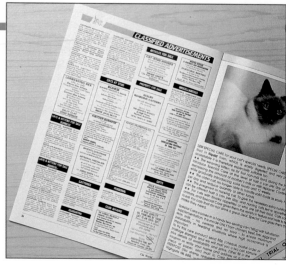

Pedigreed stud males are often advertised in cat fancy magazines (*above*) which can help you find a suitable mate for your queen. However, the original breeder, breed clubs and veterinarians may also be able to help.

Signs of pregnancy, which only become obvious in the later stages, are an enlarged abdomen and prominent breasts (*below*). Think carefully about finding homes for the kittens before you allow your cat to become pregnant.

A Cat Show (*right*) is an ideal opportunity to study prime specimens of the breed that interests you and to meet experienced breeders who will be able to offer invaluable advice and guidance.

and in the world, or the American Cat Association (ACA), which registers over 10,000 cats a year — or in one of the cat fancier magazines. These magazines will also often contain advertisements placed by the owners of stud toms. Unless you have been visiting cat shows and understand the characteristics of your breed and the faults of your particular cat or have an experienced breeder to advise you, choosing the tom will be pretty much pot luck. So long as you go to a reputable breeder, this is unlikely to matter much if you want to sell the kittens as pets rather than as potential show winners. But it is a good idea to visit the stud tom owner before your queen is in season to look at the standard of the facilities and to discuss the procedure, fees, and terms of the mating. It is normal to pay the stud fee before the mating takes place, but some agreements may allow for a second mating free of charge if the queen does not conceive after the first. Of course, you should be certain that your queen is kept indoors when she is calling, so that she is not "got at" before she visits your selected partner.

? WILL THE OWNER OF A STUD TOM NORMALLY REQUIRE ANY VACCINATIONS OR BLOOD TESTS?

Yes, hopefully. A stud tom will be visited by many queens, and could provide an ideal opportunity for the spread of infection. A stud tom owner should therefore insist on proof that visiting queens have been vaccinated against feline distemper and respiratory diseases and may well ask for the queen to be blood tested for feline leukemia virus shortly before her call to insure that she is not a carrier of that disease. Likewise, the standards of hygiene should be very high, with the pens to hold the visiting queens thoroughly disinfected.

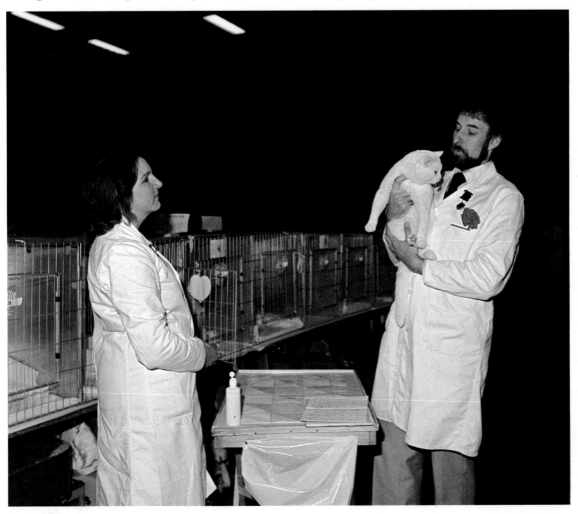

NEUTERING

The decision to "de-sex" a cat, by removing its sex organs, is an important step that a cat owner may have to face. Besides making the cat sterile, it curtails much of the more anti-social sexual behavior in both male and female cats.

? HOW CAN I TELL IF AN ADULT CAT HAS BEEN NEUTERED?

This is not too difficult with a male cat unless you happen to be presented with a cat who is an entire male but has undescended testicles, known as a *cryptorchid*. Such a cat would not have any testicles present in the scrotum and would be infertile, but would have all the behavioral characteristics of an entire tom. Fortunately, cryptorchidism is fairly rare, but bear it in mind if you have an apparently neutered male of unknown origin behaving like an entire tom.

Determining whether a female is entire can be almost impossible once the hair has regrown over the operation site after spaying. Some cat owners who take on a female cat without knowing whether or not she is neutered are happy to let her roam freely and take a chance on her becoming pregnant, or are able to keep her indoors to see if she begins to call. If, however, you do not wish to keep your new cat indoors and do not wish to enlarge your cat family any further, your veterinarian may have to carry out a spaying operation to see if the womb is present. It is possible that he may find an obvious scar in the normal operation site once the hair has been shaved, but he may have to go the whole way and operate.

? WHEN SHOULD A FEMALE CAT BE SPAYED?

Contact your veterinarian to find out when he or she prefers to carry out the operation. If you do not want your cat to have kittens, she is best spayed before she has her first season, when the womb is small and easy to remove — most veterinarians will carry this out when your kitten is around five months old. It is possible to spay a cat when she is calling, or even when she is pregnant, but the surgical risks involved are greater. If possible, she should be spayed when the womb is dormant.

? IS IT UNNATURAL FOR A FEMALE CAT TO BE SPAYED?

Yes. But the natural alternative would be for your cat to become a kitten production machine, probably producing two litters of kittens a year. In the wild, many of these kittens would not survive, but with a pet cat, the almost constant stream of

SPAYING

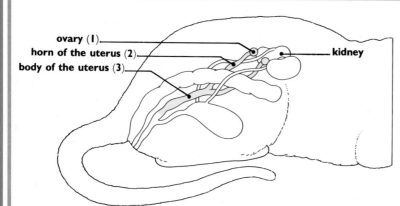

ovary (1)
horn of the uterus (2)
body of the uterus (3)
kidney

The operation is the equivalent of an ovario-hysterectomy in women and involves the removal of the female cat's sex organs — the ovaries (1), the horns of the uterus (2) and the body of the uterus (3). This may seem drastic but it is the responsible way of overcoming the problem of unwanted pregnancies and a frustrated, confined queen.

Modern anesthetics and surgical techniques make the spaying operation safe and trouble-free. The incision may be on the flank, or the midline, but is generally very small, and heals rapidly. Most cats behave as if nothing had happened within a couple of days of the operation, and after about a week the stitches are ready for removal and the hair is already beginning to regrow (*left*).

kittens would pose a great problem for the owner. Queens that are prevented from mating by being kept indoors will usually call repeatedly until irritable and exhausted; they may also develop womb infections.

CAN I PUT MY CAT ON "THE PILL" TO PREVENT HER FROM BECOMING PREGNANT?

Yes. There are drugs which can be given to prevent your cat from calling and therefore from conceiving. Some of the newer and safer drugs are given by long-acting injection rather than in tablet form. Most veterinarians prefer not to use them to postpone the first season or as a permanent alternative to spaying because of possible side-effects, but they may well be useful to delay your cat's seasons until you are ready to breed from her.

SHOULD I ALLOW HER TO HAVE ONE LITTER BEFORE SHE IS SPAYED?

If you want your cat to have a litter of kittens for the experience or because you want to keep one of her offspring, then all well and good. However, it will make no long-term difference to your cat whether she has one litter or is spayed before she begins to call, so don't do it for her sake.

WILL A SPAYED CAT STILL HAVE SEASONS?

Not normally. The ovaries are removed together with the uterus at the time of spaying, and this usually prevents her from calling. However, some spayed females do show signs of calling at certain times of the year, although they are usually very muted. This is most likely to be due to other tissues in the body producing small amounts of female hormones.

WHAT CARE WILL MY CAT NEED AFTER SPAYING?

Usually surprisingly little. Some veterinarians prefer to hospitalize all cats that have been spayed overnight, but most will allow them to return home on the same day as the operation if all is well. Follow the directions given to you when the cat is discharged and do not hesitate to telephone the vet if you are concerned. Most cats are sleepy for the first 24 hours or so after surgery, but some seem to recover remarkably quickly. Others may remain a little sleepy for a few days. Check the wound once or twice a day and contact your veterinarian if it becomes inflamed or swollen or starts to discharge. Most cats will lick at their stitches after surgery, but fortunately only a few succeed in pulling them out.

CASTRATION

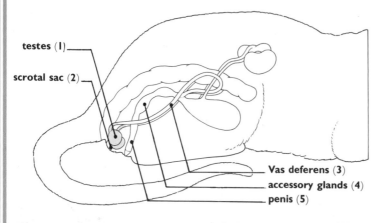

testes (1)

scrotal sac (2)

Vas deferens (3)

accessory glands (4)

penis (5)

Neutering of a male cat (*below, left*) involves the surgical removal, under anesthetic, of the male sex organs. The reproductive system of the entire male (*left*) comprises the testes (**1**) inside the scrotal sac (**2**), the tubes that carry sperm — the vasa deferentia — (**3**), accessory glands that supply fluid to the ejaculate (**4**) and the penis (**5**).

A castrated male has part of the vasa deferentia and both testes removed. A small cut is made at the base of the scrotal sac and the vasa deferentia are tied and cut. Then the testes are removed. For most tom cats, no stitches are needed. In time the scrotal sacs recede (*below, right*).

? WILL SPAYING RESULT IN ANY PERMANENT DISFIGUREMENT?

Not usually. The wound will heal and the hair will regrow over the few months after surgery. However, you may find that on a cat with colored points, such as a Siamese, the hair may regrow a darker color over the clipped area and remain that color until the cat molts, when the coat should regain its normal color. This will not worry the cat, but if you feel it may trouble you, discuss with your veterinarian the possibility of locating the incision where the discoloration will not show.

? WHY SHOULD MALE CATS BE CASTRATED?

Entire male cats, or toms, develop many characteristics which make them difficult to keep as pets. These include a much greater tendency than females or neutered males to spray urine around their territory (tom cat urine has a particularly pungent smell) and a desire to establish large territories and to defend them very aggressively against other cats. This means that tom cats are

likely to roam away from home for several days at a time and to get involved regularly in fights with other cats. This not only means that your tom cat is likely to keep getting abscesses from fight wounds, but is likely to make you somewhat unpopular with neighboring owners whose cats are getting beaten up by your tom. All cats, male or female, neutered or entire, may fight to defend their territory, but the problem is much greater with entire tom cats.

? AT WHAT AGE SHOULD A MALE CAT BE CASTRATED?

The operation can be carried out at any age, but it is usually recommended at about six months. The cat will have matured somewhat, but is unlikely to be old enough to have developed antisocial habits.

? WILL HIS NATURE CHANGE AFTER CASTRATION?

Your cat will obviously not develop the appearance and behavior of a tom cat, but neutering should not cause any change in his character as you have come to know him. Since neutered male cats are not as preoccupied about defending their territory as toms, they may become somewhat lazy and prone to put on weight. However, the vast majority of male cats kept as pets are neutered, and make very satisfactory companions.

CAN MALE CATS HAVE A VASECTOMY?

Yes — a vasectomy is an operation to tie off the tubes that carry sperm from the testes to the penis and results in the tom becoming sterile. However, there is little purpose in considering a vasectomy as an alternative to castration, since the cat will still develop all the antisocial male characteristics of a full tom. Some breeders keep a vasectomized tom to mate with queens that are in season to stop them from calling.

ARE THERE ANY POSSIBLE RISKS ASSOCIATED WITH NEUTERING?

Yes. Since both spaying a female and castrating a male cat must involve the administration of a general anesthetic, some risk exists. Complications due to a problem with the anesthetic, to bleeding directly after surgery, or to secondary infection following recovery from the operation can arise. While anyone putting their pet through any operation should be aware that there are risks, it must be stressed that routine surgery on a healthy young cat is very safe and that problems are fortunately very rare indeed. It is probably true to say that the normal risks to the health of a cat simply by going through a pregnancy are greater than the surgical risks of spaying.

SHOULD I HAVE MY CAT TATTOOED FOR IDENTIFICATION?

If possible. Tattooing is a permanent form of identification which can very easily be carried out while your cat is anesthetized for neutering — in the cat the numbers are most commonly tattooed on the ear. The main problem at present is that in the United States there is no central registry that can record identification codes for all pets. There are several commercial registration schemes. The finder of a tattooed cat may have a problem discovering where the owner has registered the number on that particular cat. An alternative is to have your zip code tattooed on the ear — an excellent solution unless you move! Tattooing is not permitted on cats that are to be shown.

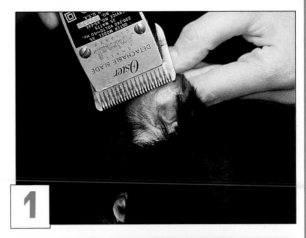

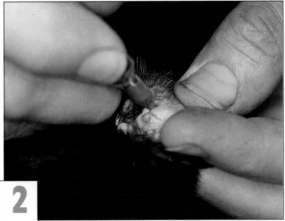

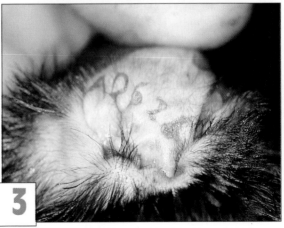

Tattooing a cat is most easily done while it is anesthetized (**1**). The hair is clipped off the inside of the ear (**2**). A dye is applied to a special tattooing gun, which actually tattoos the ear (**3**).

The ear is cleaned and the tattoo can be clearly seen. This should remain legible for the rest of the cat's life.

BASIC GENETICS

A little time spent figuring out the theoretical basis of genetics will be rewarded with a much greater understanding of the factors that control the varying external characteristics of cats.

? **WHY IS IT THAT TWO CATS WITH SHORT-HAIRED COATS CAN MATE AND PRODUCE SOME KITTENS WITH LONG-HAIRED COATS?**

In order to learn how characteristics are passed on from generation to generation it is necessary to understand a little about the principles of inheritance. In the latter half of the nineteenth century, an Austrian monk by the name of Gregor Mendel studied the inheritance of characteristics of garden pea plants. This led to the branch of biology known as *genetics* — the study of heredity. He found that the basic unit of heredity was the *gene.* Genes matche in pairs, and each pair of genes determines a different trait such as eye color, hair length and so on — although some traits such as body shape may be *multi-factorial* and controlled by several different genes. The cells responsible for reproduction, the sperm in the male and the ova in the female, each carry only one of the pair of genes for each trait so that when the two reproductive cells unite at the time of fertilization, the new cell formed has inherited half its genes from its male parent and half from its female parent. This cell then multiplies many times to form all the cells of the new kitten. Each cell contains the identical genetic code passed on from the parents to that first cell. The genetic code controls the shape and function of all the various tissues in the body.

HAIR LENGTH

A cat can be either long-haired or short-haired. There are therefore genes that we call "L" for short hair and *"l"* for long hair. A capital letter is used to denote the short-hair gene, L, because it is *dominant*

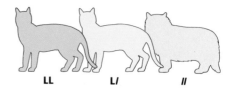
over the long-hair gene, *l,* which is therefore called a *recessive* gene. This means that if the pair of genes in the genetic material of a cat are both L, or short-hair genes, then the cat will have short hair. If both genes are *l,* or long-hair genes, then the cat will have long hair. However, if the cat has one short-hair gene, L, and one long-hair gene, *l,* it will have short hair because the short-hair gene is dominant and suppresses the long-hair gene. However, that short-haired cat will be *heterozygous* for that particular trait, and can pass on the long-hair gene to future generations. If it mates with another heterozygous short-haired cat, it can produce a long-haired kitten — quite a surprise for the owner! If, however, both genes are the same — LL or *ll* — then the cat is *homozygous* for that trait. Therefore, it follows that if a cat is long-haired, it must have homozygous long-hair genes, *ll,* but if a cat is short-haired it may be heterozygous, L*l,* or homozygous short-hair LL. There is no way to tell by looking at a short-haired cat, or in genetic terms a cat with a short-haired *phenotype*, whether it is homozygous or heterozygous for that trait — only an analysis of the offspring of that cat will reveal its hidden genetic make-up, or *genotype*.

INHERITANCE

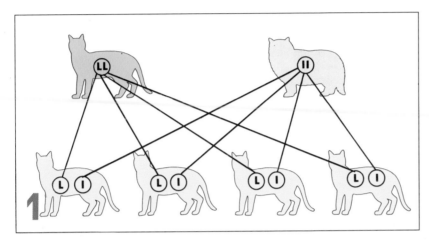

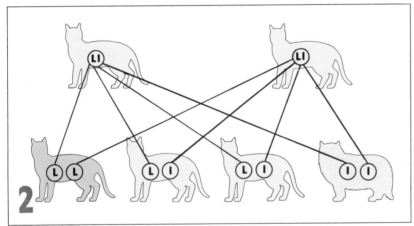

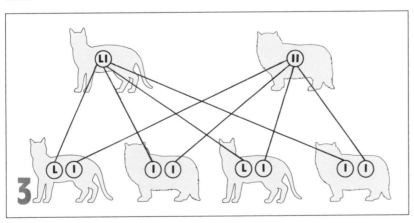

HOW SPECIFIC TRAITS ARE PASSED ON.

If a homozygous long-haired cat (*ll*) is crossed with a homozygous short-haired cat (LL), the resultant kittens will be dominantly short-haired, but will be heterozygous carriers of the long-haired gene (**1**). If two heterozygote cats (L*l*) are crossed, they will produce kittens in the ratio of three short-haired to one long-haired kind (**2**). But, if a heterozygote short-haired cat (L*l*) is crossed with a homozygote short-haired cat (LL), only short-haired kittens are produced. However one in four of the kittens will be heterozygous and carry the long-hair gene. If a heterozygote short-haired cat (L*l*) is crossed with a homozygote long-haired cat (*ll*), the cross will produce homozygote long-haired kittens and heterozygote short-haired kittens in equal proportions (**3**). If homozygotes are crossed (either LL×LL or *ll*×*ll*), they will "breed true" and produce offspring with the same trait.

In reality, if two short-haired cats are mated and produce a long-haired kitten, it becomes apparent that they must both be carriers of the long-haired recessive gene *l* — a long answer to a short question. However, understanding the theory does answer the question of how traits are passed on from generation to generation.

HOW CAN A BREEDER TELL IF A CAT IS CARRYING A PARTICULAR RECESSIVE TRAIT?

By crossing the cat with a known homozygote, that is, a cat demonstrating the recessive trait in its phenotype. It is generally accepted that if at least seven and preferably ten offspring are produced without showing the recessive trait, then that cat is a homozygote and is not carrying the recessive trait. Even if only one kitten shows the recessive trait, it is immediately known that that cat must be a heterozygote and is carrying the recessive gene.

HOW IS THE SEX OF THE KITTENS DETERMINED?

The genetic material that determines the genes is present in strands called *chromosomes*. The cells of the cat have 38 chromosomes arranged in 19 matching pairs. However, one pair of chromosomes, known as the sex chromosomes, may consist either of a matching pair of large X chromosomes if the cat is female, or a large X chromosome and a smaller Y chromosome if the cat is male. Ova from the mother always contain one X chromosome, whereas semen contains an equal number of sperm with one X and with one Y chromosome, so there is an even chance of the new offspring being either XX, and thus female, or XY, and thus male. The chance is completely random.

SEX DETERMINATION

The female ova all carry X sex chromosomes, whereas the sperm may either carry an X or a Y chromosome. If, at random, the female ova unites with a sperm that is carrying a Y chromosome, a male cat will be formed (XY). If the female ova unites with a sperm that is carrying an X chromosome a female cat will be formed (XX).

TORTOISESHELL GENETICS

The black and orange patterning on a "tortie" typically occurs in female cats with one orange (O) and one non-orange (o) gene. It is linked to sex because the genetic message associated with this trait is normally only found on the female, X, chromosome.

Males normally only possess either the orange (O) gene or the non-orange (o) gene. But, very rarely a genetic mistake occurs and a male with two X chromosomes, plus one Y chromosome crops up (XXY). If one of these X chromosomes carries the orange (O) gene and the extra X chromosome carries the non-orange (o) gene, a tortoiseshell male is produced.

ARE TORTOISESHELL CATS ALWAYS FEMALE?

Yes — or at least they are never normal males! The most common tortoiseshell coloring is a mixture of black, yellow and orange, with the addition of orange controlled by the dominant O gene. This gene is found only on the X chromosome and is therefore *sex-linked*. The tortoiseshell color is an expression of a combination of a dominant O gene for orange coloration and a recessive o gene for normal coloration (the precise color depending on other genes present). Therefore, an OO female cat will be orange (normally called red by breeders), an oo female will not have any red coloration, and an Oo female will be tortoiseshell color. Since a male cat has only one X chromosome, he can only be O — in which case he will have a red coat coloring, or o, in which case he will not have a red coat. There are a few reported cases of apparently male cats that actually have a disorder of the sex chromosomes. For example, they may have two X chromosomes and one Y chromosome. Such a cat may appear to be a male tortoiseshell but is, in fact, sterile.

ARE GINGER OR ORANGE CATS ALWAYS MALE?

No. This is a common fallacy. These cats, more correctly called red tabbies, may be male or female.

HOW DO NEW VARIETIES OF CHARACTERISTICS SUCH AS COAT COLOR COME ABOUT?

The nature of a gene may suddenly change in an individual cat by mutation, a random mistake in the order of the chemical code within the genes. These mutations occur very infrequently when embryos are developing and sometimes cause harmful disorders in the development of the animal — sometimes so harmful that the affected embryo dies or is born with congenital defects. However, on occasions, these mutations are not harmful and may result in the production of a new characteristic, such as the recessive "dilute" mutation, d, of the normal gene, D, that controls the density of hair pigmentation. For example a cat with two of these recessive genes will have a blue coat color as opposed to a black coat color for a cat with either two D genes or one of each. The dilute gene will also lighten the coat of a cat, that would otherwise be brown, to a lilac color. Therefore, the color and characteristics of a new-born kitten depend on its genetic background.

The recessive, dilute gene d, has a dramatic effect upon coat color. Chocolate, or champagne, is a brown coat color found in Burmese cats (below, top) but, if a cat that carries the same genes as a chocolate Burmese also carries two of the recessive dilute genes, the coat color will be transformed to lilac, also known as platinum (below, bottom).

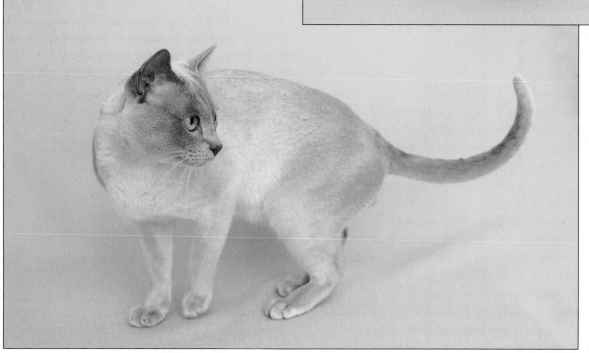

MY KITTEN HAS EXTRA TOES — IS THIS LIKELY TO CAUSE PROBLEMS?

Having extra toes, or being polydactyl, is not uncommon in cats and is due to a dominant mutant gene. It does not usually cause any problems at all.

WHY ARE THE POINTS OF A SIAMESE CAT DARKER THAN THE REST OF THE BODY?

The Siamese coloring is produced by a recessive form of the dominant C full color gene known as c^s- which produces the light-colored coat with dark points and blue eyes. The darker pigmentation at the points of the ears, legs, face and tail are due to the fact that the skin temperature is slightly lower in those places. The kittens reared in a cool environment will often grow a darker coat than those reared in a warmer environment. Similarly, bandaging part of a Siamese cat will retain body heat and make the covered area grow lighter, while clipping the hair for surgery will cool the skin by removing the insulative effect of the hair and cause new hair growth to be darker. This demonstrates how the environment can alter inherited characteristics.

WHAT IS THE ORIGINAL COAT COLOR OF THE DOMESTIC CAT?

The basic or "wild" type of coat color for a cat is the tabby. Every domestic cat is a tabby at heart, but often the tabby markings are masked with another color and are not visible. The wild or striped type of tabby marking provided the cat with excellent camouflage in its natural wooded environment. Variations on this include blotched, spotted, mackerel and Abyssinian tabbies. In the latter case, the lighter agouti color covers most of the body, and stripes are usually only visible on the face and sometimes faintly on the legs and tail. This coloring can be combined with a distinctive body type to produce the breed of cat known as the Abyssinian, but Abyssinian coloring may be found on any feline body shape. The normal agouti and black color of a tabby cat can be altered to produce variations such as blue, cream, red (ginger), or silver tabbies.

WHY DO SOLID-COLOR CATS OFTEN HAVE TABBY MARKINGS WHEN KITTENS?

This is known as *epistasis*, or masking. For example, tabby coloring is determined by the agouti gene, A, which is dominant over the non-agouti gene, a. The agouti gene produces the hairs in the lighter bands of a tabby cat. These have a black tip, a yellow band in the middle and a light-colored base. When the hairs lie against each other they produce the speckled agouti coat color — which combines with the dark bands of coat color produced by the dominant T gene and results in a tabby cat. Cats

The silver tabby was specially bred for its beauty (*above*) and is just one variation of the original brown tabby coat pattern and color, which provided an excellent camouflage.

The stripes of this self-colored kitten (*right*) will gradually fade because, although cats such as the Burmese have a "solid" coat color, they are still tabbies at heart, but with the light bands of the tabby marking, colored darkly — known as "masking."

White cats usually have orange eyes, blue eyes, or one of each — the "odd-eyed white" (*below*). Congenital deafness is most commonly seen in white cats with blue eyes.

Chinchilla coats are classically long-haired, but, the same silver hairs with black tips can be found in short-haired cats, such as in this British Tipped Shorthair (*right*).

with only one coat color genetically still have the stripes of a tabby, but the recessive non-agouti genes they carry make the pale agouti areas of the coat black. However, the striped pattern can often be seen when the cats are still kittens. There are a wide range of solid colors, including black, blue, chocolate, lilac, red and cream. Of course, many pedigreed breeds are normally solid-colored including the blue-coated British Blue, Korat and Russian Blue cats, each with its own distinctive body shape and temperament, and the popular Burmese cat, which can have a wide range of coat colors.

? IS IT TRUE THAT WHITE CATS ARE OFTEN DEAF?

Yes. White cats usually have orange eyes, blue eyes, or one of each — "odd-eyed whites". Deafness is most common in blue-eyed whites due to a degeneration of the hearing apparatus deep within the ear that develops between four and six days after birth and can affect one or both ears. The white coat color is usually due to the dominant white gene W which will mask any other colors the cat may carry in its genes, although a colored spotting can often be detected in the coat of young kittens.

? WHAT IS A CHINCHILLA CAT?

Chinchilla refers specifically to a coat color produced by white hairs with black tips. The coloring is due to the effect of a dominant inhibitor gene, I, which suppresses the development of pigment in certain areas of the cat's coat. In fact, this gene can produce differing degrees of inhibition of pigment resulting in a range of coat colors, from the almost white chinchilla coloration with only a touch of black on the tips of the hairs, through pewter, which has more black on the ends of the hairs, to the smokes with heavy coloration along most of the length of the hair but with white at the base. Cameos are red versions of this range of tipped chinchilla coat colors, and Golden Chinchillas have yellow hairs with black tips.

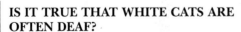

The striking coats of popular breeds are a result of a colored tip on each hair, overlying a paler underhair. Magnified hairs (*left*) show the characteristic tipping. The Chinchilla (**1**) has a modest pale tip and a slightly heavier colored tip (**2**), producing a shaded silver coat. Stripes of heavy and light pigmentation give the silver tabby effect (**3**), whereas smoke cats are produced by constant heavy pigmentation with white roots (**4**). The characteristically beautiful coat of the Golden Chinchilla is a result of black tipped yellow hairs (**5**).

? WHAT ARE REX CATS?

Rex cats have very short and curly coats due to recessive Rex genes. There are two main types of Rex gene, producing the Cornish and Devon Rex breeds, with different characteristics and hair types. The Cornish Rex was first noticed as a mutation in a kitten by the name of Kallibunker, born to a farm cat in 1951, whereas the first Devon Rex was born in 1960 to a feral curly-coated cat and named Kirlee. Each of these two kittens went on to found their respective breeds with the future generations of Devon Rexes bearing the characteristic "pixie-shaped" face that Kirlee possessed. The Rex genes can be crossed with other breeds and coat colors to produce interesting varieties such as the Si-Rex, a Rex cat with Siamese markings. Rex cats make good pets with a lively and inquisitive nature. They require very little grooming, do not shed hair about the house and may be ideal for someone who is allergic to cat hair but still wishes to keep a cat as a pet. Some breeders advise adding a little extra fat, such as shredded suet, to the diet since it is rich in calories and helps to produce the extra body heat needed to compensate for the extra heat loss due to the poor insulative qualities of their coat.

The Cornish Rex (*above*) has a long thin tail, long legs, a straight nose and a dense wavy coat — primary characteristics of the breed.

The squint, sometimes seen in Siamese cats (*right*) develops to compensate for a defect in visual signals to the brain. It is considered to be a fault in the breed.

? DO SOME BREEDS HAVE PARTICULAR GENETIC PROBLEMS?

Yes. Probably the best known example of this is the Manx cat, a very old breed with no tail. The lack of tail is due to a dominant Manx gene, M. All Manx cats are heterozygous for this gene because homozygous MM cats invariably die in the womb due to severe spinal deformities. Even heterozygous cats are often born with serious congenital abnormalities such as spina bifida.

The Scottish Fold cat has very distinctive ears which start to fold over from about four weeks of age. This is due to a dominant folded-ear gene, Fd; this gene may also cause a thickening of the tail and the legs. Due to concern about the shape of the ears causing ear problems and the thickening of the legs making movement difficult for affected cats, the Governing Council of the Cat Fancy of Great Britain decided to stop permitting registration of the breed in the 1970s. This decision was hotly opposed by breeders of Scottish Folds. The American and Australian cat societies, however, give the Scottish Fold full recognition.

? ARE SIAMESE CATS SUPPOSED TO HAVE A SQUINT?

No. The Siamese gene may cause a fault in the nervous pathways that carry messages from the eyes to the brain, and the cat may squint to try to compensate for it. It is considered a fault, as are other hereditary problems such as a "kink" in the tail and an absence of canine teeth — both of which can occur in the breed but do not seriously affect their health.

Manx cats may be completely tail-less, and known as "rumpies", with a small dimple of a tail — "rumpy-risers" (*left*), a "stumpy" with a short tail, or a "longy" with a fairly long tail.

The Peke-faced Persian (*below*) has such a flat-shaped face that eye and respiratory problems are more likely. For this reason it is not recognized as a breed in many countries.

The Scottish Fold (*bottom*) is another controversial breed. due to congential problems, with deformities of the limbs as well as the ears. It is no longer recognized in its native country, but is a fairly popular breed in the United States.

? CAN SELECTIVE BREEDING CAUSE HEALTH PROBLEMS AS IT DOES IN SOME BREEDS OF DOG?

The shape and form of the pedigreed cat remains much closer to the original wild form of cat than that of many breeds of dog. One would like to think that this is due to sensible restraint on the part of cat breeders, but, it must also be said that, pedigreed cats have been selectively bred for a much shorter time than dogs and there has been less time to produce the more extreme variations. Certainly, any highly inbred animal is likely to be less resistant to disease than one with a very wide mix of genes, and some of the effects of selective breeding may mean that the pedigreed cat will need closer attention than a mixed breed cat. For example, the long coat that has been carefully nurtured in many pedigreed Longhairs will often cause severe problems if the cat is left to its own devices to keep its own coat in order. Similarly, the "pushed-in" face of many Persian cats tends to make the eyes run due to interference with the mechanism of draining tears away from the eyes. This can usually be kept under control with regular cleaning of the eyes.

PREGNANCY

Cats cope with pregnancy well and need very little special care during this period, of about nine weeks. The signs are subtle and many cats produce litters without their owners even realizing they were pregnant.

❓ HOW LONG DOES PREGNANCY LAST?

Between 63 and 66 days on average. Larger litters tend to have shorter pregnancies, and some breeds such as the Siamese tend to have longer than average pregnancies.

❓ HOW CAN I TELL IF A CAT IS PREGNANT?

A pregnant cat will not usually begin to change shape until about six weeks into pregnancy. At three or four weeks, some reddening and swelling of the nipples may be evident. A veterinarian will be able to feel a cat's abdomen and make a fairly accurate guess as to whether she is pregnant or not, about four weeks after mating. You might like to take your cat for such an examination if you are impatient to find out, and take the opportunity to discuss how to cope with the arrival of the kittens if the pregnancy is confirmed.

❓ CAN CATS HAVE FALSE PREGNANCIES?

Yes — this may be due to a pregnancy that has been aborted or to artificial stimulation of the vagina (see p. 53). A female cat can go through all the changes of pregnancy: putting on weight, producing milk, and making a nest, and then nothing! Apart from some embarrassment at this anticlimax, most cases of false pregnancy will sort themselves out if left alone. But if there is a lot of milk, it may be necessary for your veterinarian to prescribe drugs to dry it up.

❓ IS THERE ANYTHING THAT CAN BE DONE TO TERMINATE A PREGNANCY?

There are no drugs safe enough to use to prevent conception after mating, nor is surgical abortion possible without removing the whole womb. If you wish to breed from the cat in the future, it is best to allow her to have her kittens normally. Otherwise, it is possible to spay cats two or three weeks after a season, even if pregnant. The womb will not be as small as for a routine spay, and the operative risks are therefore greater.

❓ IS THERE ANY SPECIAL DIET MY QUEEN NEEDS DURING PREGNANCY?

A pregnant queen will need a little more food in the last three weeks of her pregnancy. She may also wish to eat smaller meals more frequently than normal because the enlarged womb is restricting the space for her stomach. Be sure she receives a balanced diet (see p. 42) and let her regulate her own food intake. Some queens become constipated in the later stages of pregnancy. A little milk or oily fish may be helpful.
● Do not over-supplement the diet with vitamins.

STAGES OF PREGNANCY

Non-pregnant queen

10 to 14 days before the birth

1 to 4 days before the imminent birth

The first signs of pregnancy occur about three weeks after a female cat has mated — a "pinking up" of the nipples. Obvious signs such as a distension of the abdomen and a more restful queen only become apparent in the sixth and seventh weeks of pregnancy. During the last two or three weeks, fetal movements are visible.

HOW CAN I TELL HOW MANY KITTENS TO EXPECT?

Even your veterinarian will probably not be able to tell exactly how many kittens your cat is going to have. The average litter size is four, but it can vary from one to eight. In exceptional cases, litters of fourteen have been delivered and weaned successfully! The first litter is usually small, with the average number of kittens per litter reaching its peak at the ninth pregnancy.

IS IT SAFE FOR MY CAT TO HAVE AN X-RAY WHILE SHE IS PREGNANT?

Since there is a slight risk that an X-ray may harm the kittens, it is usually best not to X-ray a cat while she is pregnant. However, X-rays will show up kittens in the later stages of pregnancy and can be used to find out if the queen is actually pregnant or if there are any kittens left in the womb after kittening.

CAN ONE LITTER BE SIRED BY MORE THAN ONE TOM?

Surprisingly enough, yes. In *superfecundation* a queen gives birth to a litter conceived as the result of several matings by different tom cats. Since 10 percent of queens call and accept male cats while they are pregnant, it is even possible for a queen to be carrying two litters conceived at different times — most commonly about three weeks apart.

ARE THERE ANY DANGER SIGNS DURING PREGNANCY?

A slight clear discharge during pregnancy may be normal, but a blood-stained or foul smelling discharge could be a warning that abortion is occurring. The queen should be strictly confined and taken to your veterinarian. If, at any stage in the pregnancy, your cat refuses to eat and seems unwell, veterinary advice should be sought.

The skeleton of the kittens only becomes calcified and hard in the later stages of pregnancy, when radiographs can be used to look at the kittens if necessary (*left*).

A mixed litter (*above*) may occur due to genetic chance — a "throwback" — or, because it is possible for a litter to be sired by more than one tom.

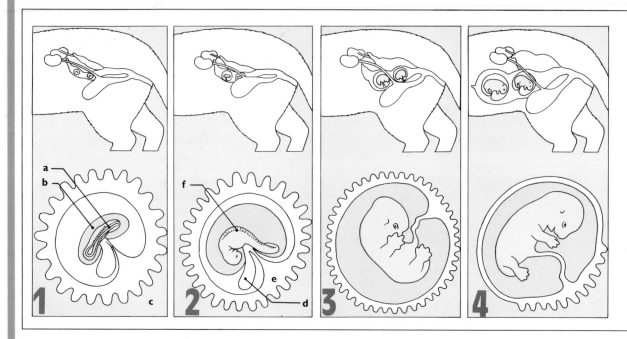

A queen can have three litters a year. However, this is likely to wear her out if continued for long, and it is preferable to restrict her to one a year.

IS IT SAFE FOR MY QUEEN TO RECEIVE MEDICATION WHILE PREGNANT?

As a general rule, it is best to avoid giving any medication that is not essential during pregnancy. Live vaccines (see p. 132) should never be given during pregnancy, and some drugs can cause congenital deformities in the kittens or abortion. Be sure that your veterinarian is aware of the likelihood that your cat is pregnant if you have to take her for treatment.

WHY IS IT THAT MY QUEEN HAS FAILED TO BECOME PREGNANT?

There are many possible causes of infertility in the cat, although the problem is not very common. Since "it takes two to make a baby", the cause may be due to problems with the male or the female. Male sterility is unlikely to be a problem with non-pedigreed cats, unless all the toms in the surrounding area have been neutered. And since a sterile stud tom is very much a matter for his owner and therefore outside the scope of this book,

we shall restrict ourselves to the causes of infertility in the female cat:

Failure to call — This may simply be due to a delayed puberty, particularly in the winter months and in female cats living alone, but there may be a physical or hormonal abnormality present. While there are drugs that can be given to try to bring the cat into heat, they are not often very effective and are usually only used in valuable queens.

Failure to mate — Uncommon in cats, failure to mate may occur in nervous queens transported to the stud tom and expected to mate immediately without being allowed to settle in. Queens that have been hand reared from a very young age may not identify with other cats socially and refuse to have anything to do with them.

Pregnancy failure — Due either to *resorption* of the dead fetuses back into the body, or to their *abortion* out of the womb, the most important causes of pregnancy failure are feline leukemia virus infection (see p.113) and *endometritis*, a bacterial infection of the womb. A blood test should be taken to rule out feline leukemia virus as a possible cause of infertility in such cases; endometritis may respond to antibiotic treatment. It is also best if the queen is allowed to call without being mated for two or three cycles. While nutritional problems and hormonal imbalances may frequently get the blame for such cases of infertility, neither seems to be a common cause.

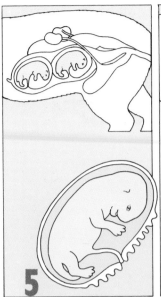
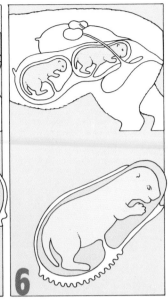

FELINE EMBRYOLOGY

Development of the unborn kittens begins 16 days after fertilization (**1**). The embryo (**a**) is surrounded by chorionic and amniotic sacs (**b**) and becomes attached to the uterine wall (**c**). A yolk sac (**d**) provides nutrients until the placenta (**e**) has developed. At 18 days (**2**) the yolk sac is shrinking and an embryonic backbone (**f**) has formed. Four days later (**3**) the embryo is receiving its nutrients from its mother across the fully developed placenta. Four weeks after fertilization (**4**) a miniature kitten of about one inch in length has developed. The fetus grows rapidly, and at five to six weeks (**5**) it reaches a length of three inches. This doubles by nine weeks (**6**), just before the kitten is born.

Pregnancy failure in a cat that has mated properly is exhibited in her behavior. The most obvious sign is a return to calling — the queen may again become extra-affectionate (*left*), start to yowl, and roll around on the floor (*above*).

BIRTH

Cats give birth naturally and usually do not need any help. In fact, the arrival of a litter usually worries the owner far more than the queen, who seems to know how to cope perfectly well — even if it is her first.

? WHAT DO I NEED TO HAVE FOR MY QUEEN BEFORE SHE GIVES BIRTH?

Provide a kittening or nesting box constructed either of wood or thick cardboard, with a hole at her waist level for her to enter, and a removable lid to facilitate observation of the kittens. It should be placed in a warm and secluded place about a week before kittening so that the pregnant queen can become accustomed to it. Newspaper makes an excellent bedding, although synthetic bedding can be purchased. The box will have to be kept warm (at least 72°F) 24 hours a day, either by keeping it in a room where the heat is kept on or by placing an electric heating pad under the box. You should also have a bag containing:

- surgical cotton swabs
- an antiseptic ointment safe for cats (see p. 142)
- petroleum jelly
- surgical scissors
- clean toweling
- strong white cotton thread
- a clean bowl ready to fill with warm water

? HOW WILL I KNOW WHEN SHE IS ABOUT TO GIVE BIRTH?

A week or so before she has her kittens, she will start to behave furtively, searching for a suitable place to have the kittens and making a nest. Two or three days before their arrival, you may notice that her abdomen "drops" and becomes noticeably pear-shaped. It may be possible to express milk from her nipples. In the last 24 hours, she will probably pace around restlessly and refuse to eat. You may then notice that straining has begun and she is actually in labor.

? WHERE SHOULD MY QUEEN HAVE HER KITTENS?

If you are lucky, your cat will adopt your box as a suitable home for her kittens — if you are less lucky it could be your new bedspread! It is best to keep her indoors in the period before she goes into labor to avoid her vanishing to get on with her job in peace behind the garden shed. Block off any inaccessible places where you don't want her to have her kittens and leave the nesting box in a quiet and sheltered place so she can discover it for herself. There is nothing more off-putting for an independent cat than to be told where to have her kittens!

? WHAT ARE THE DANGER SIGNS THAT THINGS MAY BE GOING WRONG?

If the queen produces a reddish discharge without going into labor, or if she strains strongly for more than one hour without producing any kittens, seek immediate veterinary advice.

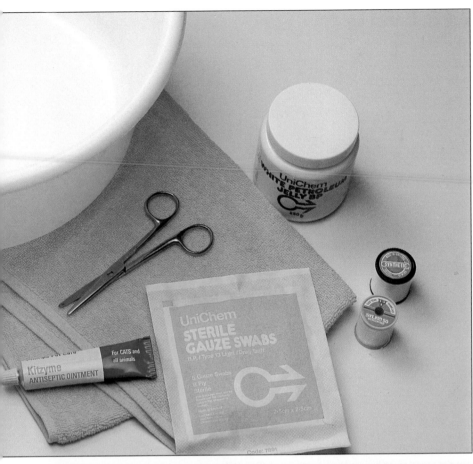

Sterilized accessories and implements (*left*) — surgical scissors, a bowl, cotton, antiseptic ointment, gauze swabs, petroleum jelly and a towel — should be at hand to help with the afterbirth. They should only be used if the queen fails to attend to the newborn kittens quickly. But, never interfere with the delivery — if there appears to be any problem, call the veterinarian.

Encourage your cat to make use of a quiet corner, ideally with a kittening box, when she begins to go into labor (*below*). However, cats that are very human-orientated may prefer to stay with the family. Beware — kittens on your blanket can be a very messy business.

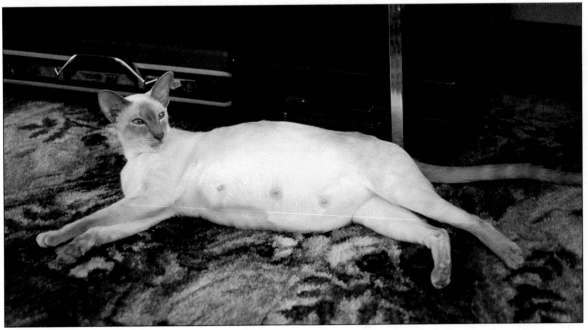

THE BIRTH

As the second stage of labor commences, (**1**), the queen will probably seek somewhere quiet and sheltered and begin to actively strain. A kitten should appear within an hour of the commencement of this active straining, (**2**), and the queen will hopefully, immediately clean up the kitten and bite off the umbilical cord. This active licking stimulates the kitten's breathing and insures that the airways are clear of mucus and fluid (**3**). More kittens may be born at further intervals, with the contraction of the womb stimulated by the suckling kittens (**4**). Finally, the fetal membranes are expelled, after each kitten has been born.

? WHAT HELP WILL SHE NEED WHILE SHE IS GIVING BIRTH?

You should keep an eye on the labor from a distance, trying to disturb the queen as little as possible. You can rest assured that the vast majority of feline births are completely routine and trouble free — unnecessary interference will only make the queen nervous and therefore complications more likely. However, some very human-oriented cats have no desire to follow the normal feline trend to "get away from it all" and are very eager to stay close to their owners when they have their kittens. Be prepared to make yourself comfortable and stay with her if she is that sort of a cat.

The fluid-filled sac around the kitten may burst before the kitten is born, or the kitten may be born still wrapped in its shiny bag. The mother will usually lick fervently at the newborn kitten and break the sac. But, particularly if it is her first litter, you may need to help clean the membranes away from the face of the kitten and wipe any fluid out from its mouth — you should, of course, always wash your hands before handling the kittens. The birth process may be fairly slow, so do not rush to pull on a kitten that is half-presented. Watch from a distance, and only help if it is obvious that the mother is getting nowhere with her own contractions, and the kitten appears stuck. In this case, you should clear the membranes away from the kitten's mouth so that it can breathe and pull

FETAL POSITIONS

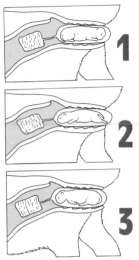

In terms of ease of labor, the optimum position for the kitten to be in at birth is anterior, head first, and this is the most common situation (**1**). Problems may occur if the kitten happens to be in the posterior, feet first, position (**2**) but only if the queen weakens. The most difficult position is the true breach (**3**), when the kitten emerges hindquarters first.

The mother cat is contented and happy after the kittens have been born and the members of the new family spend their days alternately feeding and sleeping. Each kitten will show a preference for a specific nipple soon after it is born and return to its "own" one at feeding times.

downward gently on the kitten as the queen contracts.

- Do not use excessive force when assisting both and obtain veterinary advice if you are not rapidly successful.
- Do not worry if the hind leg appears first, this is perfectly normal and can usually be coped with unassisted.

THE BIRTH

Most kittens will start to move and to cry soon after birth. If the mother is not cleaning a kitten properly and it is not obviously moving and breathing, you may need to pick it up and rub it vigorously in a rough towel to stimulate it. If this doesn't do the trick, try holding the kitten in the palm of your hand and gently but firmly swinging the hand downward and then back up again. Be careful — newborn kittens are as slippery as a bar of soap. Keep the kitten's head lower than the rest of its body so that any fluid in its airways can drain down and out of the mouth. Here the bowl of warm water may be vital. Immersing its body in warm water is the quickest way to warm up a kitten that may have become chilled. If the mother is not taking much notice of the kittens, perhaps distracted by the birth process, the kittens should be kept covered in a box on a warm hot water bottle wrapped in a blanket. The mother will usually bite through the umbilical cord attaching the kitten to its placenta. There is no rush to separate the placenta but if it remains attached after a few minutes it can be severed with your fingers, about two inches from the kitten, or cut with surgical scissors that have been cleaned with disinfectant. The remaining length of cord will shrivel and drop off the kitten within a few days. Breaking the cord too near the kitten may cause bleeding, or an *umbilical hernia*. If the umbilical cord bleeds excessively when it is broken, it can be tied off with some strong cotton thread.

If the queen is unable to pass a kitten, and strains hard for more than an hour, seek veterinary advice — but remember, it is not unusual for there to be a gap of several hours, or even days in rare cases, between kittens delivered normally. If a queen strains firmly at first, but does not produce a kitten, and then gradually strains infrequently and half-heartedly, she may be going into *uterine inertia*, where the womb becomes tired and unable to contract properly. Most such cases respond well to drugs that your veterinarian can give to stimulate the womb. If you are in doubt, seek advice too soon rather than too late. Don't panic if the mother decides to make a meal of the placentas.

CARE OF KITTENS

How to make the most of rearing your kittens — they develop into cats surprisingly fast — and some tips on health care, dietary matters and helping the mother.

? WHAT CAN I DO IF MY QUEEN ATTACKS HER KITTENS?

Being a mother comes very naturally to most cats, but occasionally one may panic and start to injure or even kill one or more of her youngsters. Immediately separate her from any injured kittens. Hold her and comfort her until she seems calm; then try to introduce her to her unharmed kittens again but do not leave her alone with them until all has been well for several hours. If she starts to attack them again, contact your veterinarian to see if a tranquilizer is called for — you might well need one too by that time! Even then, some female cats cannot adjust to raising a family, and hand rearing the kittens becomes the only alternative (see p.81).

? WHAT CAN I DO IF MY QUEEN REJECTS SOME OR ALL OF HER KITTENS?

Often, a litter contains one or two kittens that are smaller and weaker than the rest. They are known as runts. It is possible that these kittens have congenital defects, and it is not uncommon for a queen to ignore them and fail to look after them properly. It is important to ensure that such kittens are kept warm and are able to compete with the stronger kittens for a place on the nipple. Supplementary feeding may be necessary. Some of these kittens will fail to thrive and will die, despite the closest attention, but some will survive, and although they usually remain small and less sturdy than their siblings, they often grow up to be loving and affectionate pets, perhaps partly due to the extra human contact they had when they were young.

? IS THE QUEEN LIKELY TO HURT THE KITTENS BY HANDLING THEM TOO ROUGHLY?

No, unless she is one of the few queens that makes a conscious decision to injure her kittens. This is most likely to occur immediately after they are born. Although it may appear that she picks them up somewhat roughly, she will not harm them. She will normally pick them up by the scruff, but some feline mothers develop their own methods, such as the "head in the mouth technique" — guaranteed to give owners palpitations!

? HOW CAN I TELL IF THE KITTENS HAVE ANY CONGENITAL PROBLEMS?

While there is a wide range of serious abnormalities that can be present at birth, they are fairly rare. If the disorder is very serious, the kitten

Close contact with the queen is important for insuring that the kittens are kept warm (*left*). Most queens are very good at keeping an eye on all the litter, but watch out for any smaller kittens that may be rejected.

The natural way for a queen to carry her kittens is by the scruff of the neck (*below*). It may not appear very comfortable but it will not cause the kittens any harm.

may be born dead or die soon after birth. One of the most frequent problems is *cleft palate*. The roof of the mouth fails to fuse together properly, so a hole is present from the mouth up into the nose. This prevents the kitten from suckling properly, and milk may actually be seen to run down the nose. Affected kittens are probably best put to sleep painlessly by your veterinarian. *Umbilical hernias* are also quite common and can be recognized as a soft swelling around the "belly-button" where the umbilicus entered the abdomen. Unless they are very large, they do not usually cause any problems.

 IS IT POSSIBLE FOR MY KITTENS TO PICK UP INFECTIOUS DISEASES FROM THEIR MOTHER?

When they are born, the kittens will have *maternal antibodies* in their blood. These are passed from the mother's blood to the kittens' while they are in the womb, and are also in the milk the kittens suckle for the first day or two after they are born. These antibodies will protect the kittens against all the diseases that the mother has formed a protection against. Over the first few weeks of life, the amount of maternal antibodies in the blood of the kittens slowly decreases until the kittens have lost all their protection and are susceptible to disease. The stress of giving birth and rearing kittens may cause the queen to start to excrete 'flu viruses that were dormant in her body until then. These can then be passed on to the kittens when their immunity wanes. In most cases, this will cause only mild symptoms in the kittens. But if a queen is known to be a 'flu virus carrier, it may be advisable to wean the kittens early and separate them from their mother.

? **HOW SHOULD THE KITTENS BE WEANED?**

Weaning from milk to solid foods can commence as soon as the kittens are able to stand — usually at around five weeks of age — but should be carried out gradually. It may be possible to get the kittens to lap milk even earlier by encouraging them to lick milk off your finger and then putting your finger into the milk so they continue to lap from the bowl. Then thicken plain milk (ideally with a commercial formulation especially for kittens, or alternatively, three parts evaporated milk with one part boiled water) with a zwieback. All foods should be fed at body temperature to kittens at this stage. The kittens can be introduced gradually to scraped beef or finely mashed up canned kitten food a little at a time. The kittens should then start to feed themselves regularly and will probably only suckle from their mother occasionally for comfort, especially at night. Given the chance, kittens will often continue to suckle until they are several months old, and mother will obligingly continue to produce milk. Some feline mothers appear to become tired of feeding their young when they are a few weeks old and refuse to allow them to suckle. If you are keeping some of the kittens yourself, you may have to separate the queen from her kittens entirely for a while.

? **WHEN CAN MY QUEEN BE SPAYED AFTER HAVING KITTENS?**

Discuss this with your veterinarian, but don't leave it for too long unless you want another family of kittens to look after. Most cats will not start to call while they are still feeding their young, but some queens will come into season surprisingly soon after the kittens are born. If this happens, she should be kept away from entire tom cats. It is safest to keep a queen with her litter away from other cats anyway, to prevent the spread of infection. Most veterinarians prefer to wait until the queen's milk has dried up before she is spayed.

The weaning process can gradually begin as the kittens reach four or five weeks of age, and begin to become more independent (*left*). It is best to wean them onto milk first — a commercial feline milk replacement is better than cow's milk, and then onto finely minced or scraped meat. It is important to remember that the stomach of a kitten is very small, so they will need to be fed small amounts, frequently.

DAILY FOOD INTAKE

Age in weeks	Mother's milk	Number of milk feeds	Number of solid feeds	Size of each feed in teaspoons
0—3	Yes	0	0	—
3—4	Yes	3	0	½—1
4—5	Yes	3	1	1—2
5—6	Yes	2	2	2—3
6—8	Yes	2	2	3
8—12	Maybe	2—3	2	3—4
12—16	No	2	3	6—8
16—24	No	1	2	9—12
over 24	No	0	2	c12

You can either use milk specially formulated for kittens, powdered milk for babies — made up in the correct way, or, a mixture of three parts unsweetened evaporated milk to one part of boiled water. Early feeds should be at body temperature. Gradually the kittens can be weaned on to solid foods.

GROWTH AND DEVELOPMENT

The newborn kitten should be able to propel itself along the ground with its legs, search for the teat and begin to feed within an hour or two after birth. Its eyes are firmly shut and its ears closed, but it has a keen sense of smell and is very sensitive to touch. For the first few days the queen will hardly leave the nest at all. Her licking and grooming of the kittens is very important to keep them clean and to stimulate them to empty their bowels and bladder.

By the end of the first week the kittens should have doubled their birth weight. Their eyes may be starting to open (the eyes of some breeds, such as Siamese, may open a few days after birth), and the stumps of the umbilical cord will have shriveled up and dropped off. While they are still not able to walk, they can pull their legs underneath themselves and crawl, using their legs as paddles.

At two weeks of age the eyes should be fully open and the ears starting to prick up.

By three weeks of age the kittens can stand and walk, somewhat unsteadily. If an eye does not appear to be opening properly, and particularly if there is a thick discharge, seek veterinary advice, since an eye infection in such young kittens can easily cause permanent eye damage. Teeth begin to grow at this age, and you may start to wean the kittens, particularly if the litter is large.

By the time the kittens are six weeks old they are very much little individuals, able to run, climb, play and get into mischief. They explore their surroundings eagerly at this age, and socialization with people and other animals such as dogs is vital if they are to accept them readily when they are adult. The kittens are able to groom themselves and demand food, and they should be well on the way to being weaned. Once they are fully weaned, they can go to their new homes — if their owner can bear to part with them!

A new born kitten has closed eyes and tiny folded-down ears.

After a week, the eyes have opened.

At two weeks of age, the kitten is becoming sturdier and beginning to crawl.

By three weeks, the kitten can stand, unsteadily, and the ears have straightened up.

By six weeks the kitten is sturdy, mischievous and is able to feed and groom itself.

To conserve their body heat, the kittens huddle together closely (*right*). If the kittens are too warm, they will spread out to become cooler. An infra-red lamp suspended above the kittening box is an ideal means of heating, since it enables the kittens to find the spot with the temperature that they find most comfortable.

HOW CAN I GO ABOUT FINDING HOMES FOR THE KITTENS?

There is no hard and fast rule as to how old the kittens must be before they are sent to new homes, but they should be able to cope well with solid food before they are separated from their mother. You will probably have given some thought to finding owners for the kittens before deciding to allow your queen to breed. As soon as you know how many kittens have been born, you should start to arrange for their future homes. It is obviously best if you can find homes through personal contacts, but it is possible to display an advertisement in a drugstore, supermarket or pet shop. Your veterinarian may be willing to allow you to display a notice in his waiting-room — some keep a record of kittens that are looking for homes so they can pass the information on to any potential new owners. Local animal shelters may also be willing to assist, but it is far better for the kittens to go directly from your home to their new owner. They should not be passed on for sale by a pet shop or sent to a home for stray animals unless there is absolutely no alternative. It is stressful enough for a kitten to have to go to one new home without changing hands again, and if it is mixed with other cats and kittens, it may well contract a disease.

HOW DIFFICULT IS IT TO HAND REAR KITTENS?

Hand rearing a litter of kittens from birth may be necessary if the mother is ill or injured and is unable to provide milk, but this is a demanding task and should not be embarked upon lightly. If at all possible, the kittens should be kept with their mother, so that she can attend to grooming and toilet-training, and provide all the warmth and feline contact her kittens need. A medicine bottle

HAND REARING

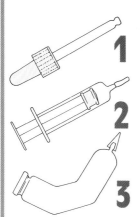

As a makeshift measure, a dropper (**1**) or a syringe (**2**) can be used to feed the kittens (*above*). But, once the kittens are able to suckle strongly, a proper feeding bottle and teat designed for kittens should be used (**3**). Insure that you only feed slowly, so that milk is not inhaled by accident. In the case of very young, weak kittens, your veterinarian may be able to show you how to use a stomach tube for feeding.

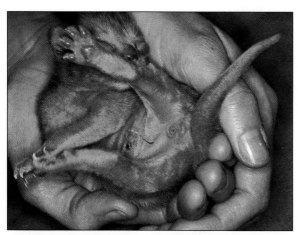

A newborn kitten (*above*) can easily be cupped in the palm of one's hand, but should not normally need to be picked up and the mother may become agitated and aggressive if her kittens are handled unnecessarily.

or a syringe can be used as a stop-gap aid in feeding newborn kittens, but special kitten feeding bottles are now available and should be purchased either from your veterinarian or from a pet shop. Three parts evaporated milk with one part boiled water can be fed, but again, a commercial product designed specifically for milk replacement in cats is much better. It is available under the brand name of Bordens Esbilac in the United States. Hand reared kittens must be kept very warm at all times — about 86°F initially, cooling gradually to about 70°F at six weeks — either by keeping the room they are in at a constant temperature, or by using an infra-red heat lamp. If the kittens are warm, they will lie sprawled out in their nest area, but if they are cold, they will all huddle together near to any heat source. It is important to assist with urination and defecation by rubbing the area around the anus gently with cotton after feeding, although the first movement may not be passed until about four days after birth. Hand reared kittens should be weighed regularly to check that they are getting enough food — a weight gain of about one-third of an ounce per day is satisfactory. While completely hand reared kittens will not have had the chance to gain the full amount of protection from disease by drinking their mother's milk soon after birth, it is nevertheless important that they socialize with other healthy, vaccinated cats while they are still quite young if they are to grow up to identify with other cats at all. Although hand rearing very young kittens is an exhausting and time-consuming task, it is often very rewarding, since the kittens usually respond to the extra human contact by growing up to become exceptionally affectionate cats. With large litters, it may be necessary to supplement the occasional feed with a milk substitute, especially for the weaker kittens that may not be getting a chance to feed properly.

? IS IT POSSIBLE TO FOSTER ABANDONED KITTENS ONTO ANOTHER QUEEN?

Yes. In fact, queens that live together will often "pool" their kittens if they are born at around the same time, so it is not difficult to add one or two kittens to a litter while the mother is out of the room. The kittens will soon pick up the smell of the other kittens and should not be noticed by the queen when she returns. Fortunately arithmetic is not a strong subject in the feline world! If you do not know of a suitable foster mother, it may be worth contacting your veterinarian to see if he can help you to find one.

ON THE MOVE

Cats are easier to transport if they become accustomed to traveling when they are young. Even so, many cats do not take kindly to it, but there are times when it is essential.

? IS IT WISE TO LEAVE MY CAT AT HOME WHEN I GO ON VACATION?

Some cats are quite relaxed about who looks after them, but most cats do get pretty attached to their own surroundings and dislike being moved out of their familiar environment. Therefore, if you are able to get someone to live in your home while you are away or can arrange for someone to stop by to check and feed your cat two or three times each day, your cat will probably be less upset than it would be if you moved it to strange surroundings. Your cat may not even notice that you've gone! An arrangement like this however, may only be less stressful for the cat if you are away for a short period only. Otherwise boarding is preferable because the cat may receive more attention.

? WHAT CAN I DO IF MY CAT NEEDS TO BE GIVEN REGULAR TREATMENT?

Most boarding homes will oblige and administer medicines prescribed by your veterinarian if arranged in advance. Of course, it may be necessary for them to call in their own veterinarian at your expense to examine your cat if complications develop while you are away. It can be a major problem when cats decide to fall ill just before you are due to go on vacation. If the problem requires more supervision than a boarding home could be expected to cope with, your veterinarian may be able to look after the cat for you at his office and administer treatment as necessary, or he may be able to refer the cat to a veterinary hospital with facilities for sick animals.

? IS IT A GOOD IDEA TO TAKE CATS AWAY ON VACATION?

Cats generally travel well and settle into new surroundings quickly if they have been used to traveling regularly since they were young. It is important that the cat not be allowed to escape, for if your cat runs off in unknown territory, he will possibly be lost for good. Cats that travel with their owners will often accept restraint with a harness and leash.

• It is wise to check on any local restrictions on the movement of animals before you travel.

? HOW CAN I CHOOSE A BOARDING HOME?

Personal recommendation is always the best. Speak to friends that have boarded their cats and find out which they would recommend. Do not be afraid to telephone the boarding home and ask to be shown around. Be sure that the facilities look clean and well-maintained and that boarded cats are not allowed to come into contact with each other and spread disease. If the cat is being boarded for any length of time, it is best for each pen to have its own indoor or outdoor run, which again should be separated by a solid divide from other runs, or have a space of at least two feet between each one. Your veterinarian may be prepared to assist you in your choice, but remember that while he or she may recommend a place in good faith, problems

Harnesses are more secure than collars, and should be made of soft leather or nylon, fully adjustable to fit snugly (*right*). It is best to get the cat used to wearing the harness at home first, and after a few days start to attach a leash and accustom the cat to being led. Only venture into quiet areas initially and tackle busy streets when the cat accepts the restraint readily.

can arise even at the best-run establishments. The Cat Fanciers' Association (CFA) and similar organizations (see p.17) lay down a very high standard for approved boarding homes and can supply an address list on application. In some countries, notably the United Kingdom, catteries have to pass an inspection by the local authority, so the claim "Approved" does not mean much, except that they meet the minimum legal requirements.

? WILL MY CAT NEED TO BE VACCINATED?

Yes. Any boarding home worth its salt will insist that all cats are up to date with infectious enteritis and cat 'flu vaccinations — you should be warned of this when you make your reservation. If your cat is going to be almost due for its booster when it goes in, it is wise to have it boosted before it goes in, in order to give maximum protection. Be sure your "Record of Vaccination" has been brought fully up to date by your veterinarian.

? WHAT SHOULD I TAKE WITH MY CAT TO THE BOARDING HOME?

Take the cat along in a sturdy cat carrier (see p. 87) and remember your "Record of Vaccination" if you have not already been asked to show it. Bring any toys that your cat is fond of and any blanket or similar bedding that is familiar to your cat. Don't forget to take along any necessary medications.

An outdoor cattery is a wired enclosure that allows cats the freedom of the fresh air, without the risk of injury of escape. Ideally, it should be connected to a shelter with the cat's bed and food (*above*).

Cats accustomed to walking on a leash can be taken out and about with the owners regularly (*right*) and exercised in unfamiliar areas — a cat without a leash would simply run off and hide.

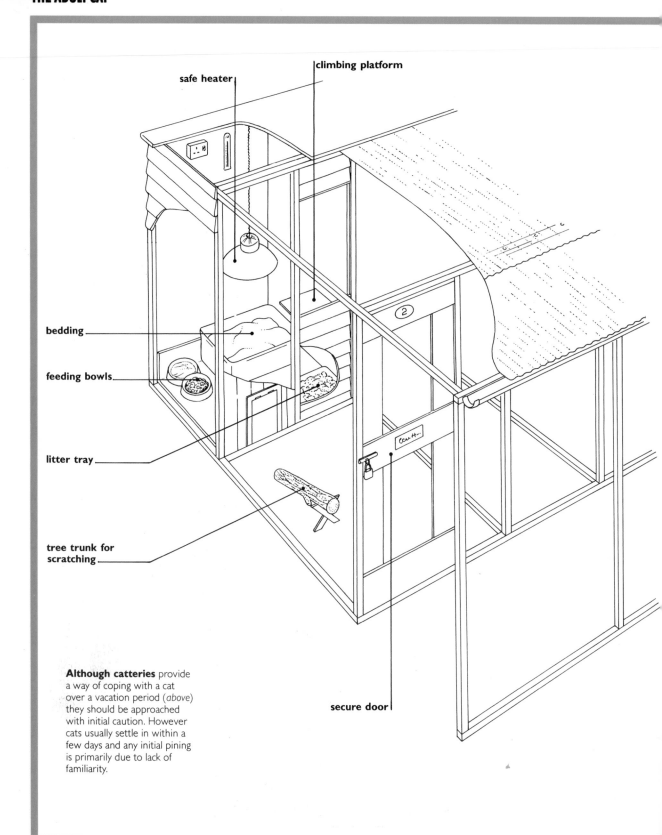

safe heater

climbing platform

bedding

feeding bowls

litter tray

tree trunk for
scratching

secure door

Although catteries provide
a way of coping with a cat
over a vacation period (*above*)
they should be approached
with initial caution. However
cats usually settle in within a
few days and any initial pining
is primarily due to lack of
familiarity.

WHAT POINTS SHOULD I LOOK OUT FOR IF I GO TO VISIT A BOARDING HOME?

Security — Obviously each pen must be escape-proof. Also, the entrance to each pen should not be open to the outdoors — in other words, there should be at least two doors between the cat and the big wide world.

Shelter — Pens should be large enough for the cat to move around comfortably and ideally should have access to an outdoor run. It is essential that each cat be kept completely isolated from other cats at all times (except when more than one cat from the same household are boarded together). Supplementary heating is necessary in winter.

Hygiene — All surfaces should be easily cleanable and should be kept clean and in good order.

Tender loving care — This is obviously an extremely important requirement. The ideal boarding home owner will take great pride in the running of the home and caring for each cat individually. He or she will be eager to discover the likes and dislikes of each boarder and will always be on the look-out for signs of trouble.

 WHAT IF MY CAT SHOULD BECOME ILL WHILE I AM AWAY?

Every boarding home should have an arrangement with a local veterinarian for the care of their boarders. You will probably be asked to sign a form to authorize the home to arrange for any essential treatment, although they will probably try to contact you first if possible. It is normal for any such costs to be borne by the owner, but it may be possible to take out insurance while the cat is boarded to cover veterinary fees. If your cat has received treatment recently, be sure the home has the telephone number of your own veterinarian to enable him to find out details of previous treatment given if the need should arise — a letter outlining any treatment given should then be passed on to your veterinarian when the cat is picked up from the home.

 WHAT IF I AM DISSATISIFIED WITH THE CARE MY CAT HAS RECIEVED AT A BOARDING HOME?

First of all discuss it with the home concerned. If the cat is unwell, it should be examined by your own veterinarian and his advice sought. It is possible for a cat to fall ill even at the best run homes, and you only have grounds for complaint if you can prove that the home did not provide a reasonable standard of care in the circumstances. Most cases of dissatisfaction can be worked out amicably between the parties concerned. Only in the most extreme cases is it necessary to seek legal advice. Naturally, if you are not entirely happy with the state of your cat when you arrive home even after taking the matter up with the boarding home owner, you should not take your cat back there in future.

Boarded cats (*left*) should not come into contact with other cats at the boarding home. If the chalets have outside runs, they should either have solid partitions, or should have a space of at least three feet between them. All the surfaces should be easily cleanable, and the cat should have some sort of ledge that it can climb up onto. Heating is essential in areas where the temperature may drop, and a cleanable bed should be available, with suitable bedding. It is a good idea to take along any familiar, personal bedding or toys.

Traveling in cars is easier for cats if they are first taken out when young (*below*). Insure that the cat is properly restrained when the vehicle is in motion, or it may pose a dangerous distraction to the driver.

HOW CAN I STOP MY CAT FROM RUNNING OFF JUST AFTER MOVING HOME?

This is not usually as much of a problem as people expect. Keep your cat indoors for a few days after moving, until it seems settled in the new surroundings. When you do let your cat outdoors, time it so that it goes outdoors just before feeding time — your cat should soon be back for dinner! Cats are generally very cautious about exploring new territory and will not usually venture far afield until they are familiar with the lie of the land. Buttering the paws is a popular old wives' tale — it doesn't make much difference to the cat and certainly plays havoc with the new rug.

SHOULD CATS BE SEDATED FOR TRANSPORT?

Cats seem to react strangely to many drugs, and some sedatives seem to have the opposite effect in a few cats. Therefore, many veterinarians are reluctant to give sedatives to cats. If they are prescribed, it is probably best to try them out on a "dummy run" before you set out on a long day's journey with an hysterical cat in the rear. If a cat is not used to traveling in a car, it is important to carry it in a large, sturdy carrying box with plenty of clean newspaper in it.

● Do not feed the cat before you set out, but be sure that fresh water is available from time to time.
● Do not leave the car parked in the sun with the cat locked inside.

WHAT SHOULD I DO IF I WISH TO TAKE MY CAT WITH ME WHEN I MOVE ABROAD?

It is essential that you check the import regulations of the country to which you are traveling well before you depart. You may find that most, if not all countries have requirements such as a rabies vaccination given at least one month before the cat enters the country. The best place to contact initially for information is the local office of the United States Department of Agriculture where you will be guided to the right channel. An official health certificate should, as a rule, be no more than five days old and sometimes has to be translated into the language of the country in question and notarized by the consulate. Very often, this procedure is extremely complicated and time-consuming. Remember that a rabies vaccination is required for all travel abroad and is necessary for re-entry into the United States. In fact, cats that are allowed outside should be vaccinated every year.

❓ WHAT VACCINATIONS WILL MY CAT NEED?

This will depend very much on the country to which you are traveling — the most common vaccinations are for rabies, distemper and upper respiratory infections. In any case, consult your veterinarian well ahead of time, as well as your local office of the United States Department of Agriculture.

❓ WHAT CONTAINER SHOULD MY CAT TRAVEL IN?

For traveling with your pet by 'plane, train or bus, you should request the transportation regulations as well as the size and type of container that can be used ahead of your travel date. Various types of containers are available for air travel, depending on the company. While a special type of carrier may not be essential if you travel by other means, such as by boat, CFA approved carriers are nevertheless probably advisable for your cat.

A sturdy carrier (*top*) is essential for cats that are not used to traveling, and for nervous cats sedation may be advisable for long journeys.

Most airlines abide by the International Air Travel Association for the transport of animals, and may well insist on a standard size and design of carrier for cats (*above*).

FERAL CATS

Statistically, little is known about the free-roaming communities of stray cats that successfully survive on the outskirts of farms and cities. However, recent research provides new clues to their lifestyle and habits.

Crush cages with collapsible sides (*above*) are used to transport feral cats so that they are only subjected to minimum handling and distress. They are captured humanely using modern cat traps.

Semi-wild, stray or feral cats usually live on the edges of human habitation or on derelict sites (*right*). Destruction of such cats is often carried out, but simply results in rapid re-colonization of the site by other cats.

? WHAT IS A FERAL CAT?

A feral cat is a domestic cat that has adapted to living in the wild. They generally live on the fringes of human habitation, and while counting the feral cat population would be an impossible task, some estimates put the total at about 12 million in the United States.

? IS THERE ANY HARM IN FEEDING FERAL CATS?

As in most wild animal populations, the number of feral cats in a given area will depend mainly on the food resources available. Cats can reproduce very rapidly and when there is insufficient food, those that are unable to compete either move off to new territory or starve. Therefore, it is probably best not to interfere with the balance of nature by regularly feeding feral cats. If you are suddenly unable to continue to feed them, you will upset the balance that has been established and some cats may die. Additionally, an artificially high density of cats in an area may promote the spread of disease from cat to cat. Of course, if there is very severe weather or a sudden cut-off of their normal supply of food, it is perfectly acceptable to leave food out on a temporary basis.

? DO FERAL CATS POSE A HEALTH RISK?

No. They may cause a nuisance by rummaging through trash bins and by fighting or serenading at night, but it is most unlikely that they will pass any diseases on to humans. In fact, by keeping the numbers of rodents down, they probably help to prevent the spread of disease.

? HOW CAN I ARRANGE TO CATCH FERAL CATS FOR NEUTERING OR TREATMENT?

Special cat traps are available for the capture and handling of feral cats. Commercial firms can be employed to trap and neuter cats, or the assistance of animal welfare organizations may be sought. It will probably be necessary to accustom the cats to receiving food in one spot for several nights before setting a trap in that position. Cat traps should either be checked regularly throughout the night, or covered in plastic to keep off rain, which can soak and severely chill a trapped cat unable to seek shelter.

? CAN FERAL CATS BE DOMESTICATED AND KEPT AS PETS?

With difficulty. Cats that live on rough ground away from humans are unlikely to be trainable, but cats that are used to living near houses and being fed there may gradually allow themselves to be approached. A young feral cat can be conditioned to tolerate and even enjoy human attention.

? WHO IS RESPONSIBLE FOR THE CONTROL AND TREATMENT OF FERAL CATS?

Nobody — wild animals have no legal owners. However, most animal welfare organizations, such as the American Society for the Prevention of Cruelty to Animals (ASPCA), will assist with the costs of essential treatment if the need arises.

? WHAT IS THE IDEAL WAY TO CONTROL COLONIES OF FERAL CATS?

Unless they are seriously ill, it should not be necessary to destroy feral cats — their place will soon be taken by other cats anyway. The best means of controlling the number of feral cats is to trap and neuter them. It is now standard practice to "ear tip" feral cats that have been neutered so that they are not captured again for neutering. It is possible to put contraceptive drugs into the cats' food, but it is impossible to insure that each cat obtains the correct dose on a regular basis, and surgical neutering is far preferable.

EAR TIPPING

While under anesthetic for neutering, some feral cats have the tip of the left ear removed. This enables easy identification once the cat is released and prevents the same cat being re-captured for neutering at a later date.

THE ELDERLY CAT

3

A cat kept lovingly in your home will live to be much older than a cat living in the wild, and may, therefore, need rather special care and attention in later years. As in humans, the onset of the signs of old age may vary tremendously — some cats may be showing distinct signs of old age at 12 whereas others are still behaving like kittens at 16. An elderly cat might require special care and an owner can learn to recognize some of the diseases which are common in old age, and even learn to diagnose some of the common problems in their early stages. Ultimately, the question of euthanasia arises and this is a problem that many pet owners may have to tackle.

Relaxing and sleeping become important pastimes for older cats and, in a typical way, this brown tabby (*right*) has chosen a warm and cozy spot.

LOOKING AFTER AN ELDERLY CAT

Although an elderly cat may not be very active, he or she may still give you several more years of pleasure.

? HOW LONG CAN I EXPECT MY CAT TO LIVE?

While a feral cat will be lucky to live to the age of 10 years, pet cats have a considerably longer life expectancy. The "normal" lifespan is about 14 years, but it is not unusual for cats to live to be 16 or 17 years old. Cats that survive even longer than that are the exception rather than the rule, but cats of over 20 years are reported fairly regularly. The absolute maximum lifespan for a cat is between 25 and 30.

? WHAT SIGNS MAY I NOTICE WHEN MY CAT GETS OLD?

Many cats are surprisingly resistant to the effects of old age, but you will probably find that your cat will gradually become less active and sleep for long hours in a favorite warm spot. Some cats may put on weight, but most older cats tend to slowly lose weight and may well develop an increased thirst. Failing eyesight and deafness are common in old cats but do not necessarily mean that the cat has to be put to sleep. With a little extra care and attention, such cats can learn to cope very well in familiar surroundings.

? WHAT EXTRA CARE WILL MY ELDERLY CAT NEED?

Regular veterinary check-ups are a good idea to pick up problems early. Many elderly cats will need more grooming than when they were younger and will be less able to cope with the hair they swallow. The nails of an elderly cat may well overgrow, even to the point where they begin to curl around and grow back into the pads of the feet

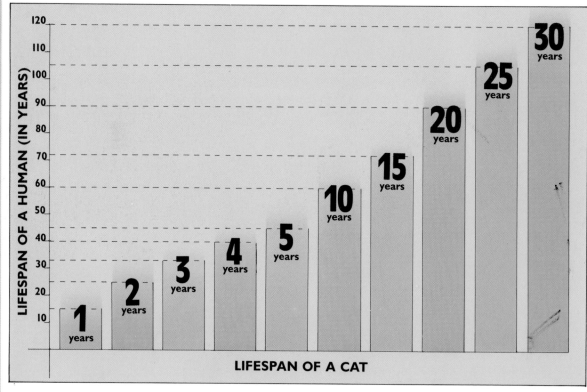

OVERGROWN CLAWS

Elderly cats may not wear down their nails by scratching and climbing, and they may overgrow, even to the point where they curl around and grow into the toe (*far left*). It is important to keep an eye on the nails, and clip them before they become overlong, taking care not to cut into the sensitive pink quick (*left*).

again. If necessary, they should be regularly clipped well before they reach that state. Be sure that your elderly cat has a warm and draft-free bed to go to and try to discourage him from staying outside for too long in very cold weather. Older cats will often drink more water than when they were younger, and a plentiful supply of fresh water must be available at all times.

 IS THERE ANY SPECIAL DIET I SHOULD FEED MY CAT WHEN HE GETS OLDER?

While many cats are pretty fussy eaters at the best of times, you can probably expect your cat to become even more choosy in his eating habits as he ages. Good quality, easily digested sources of protein should be fed, such as fish, rabbit, chicken and cooked eggs, together with a reputable balanced mineral supplement. If your cat is losing weight, you should try to encourage him to eat starchy foods as well as meat. This is not very popular with many cats, but you could experiment with foods such as rice, pasta with butter, bread and butter, potato chips and potatoes. Older cats will often want to eat smaller and more frequent meals, and should be fed on demand.

A direct comparison between the age of a cat and that of a human (*left*) is difficult to make because the rate of aging slows down as the cat gets older. The first year is roughly equivalent to 15 human years but, in the later years of life, each cat year is only comparable to about 3 human years.

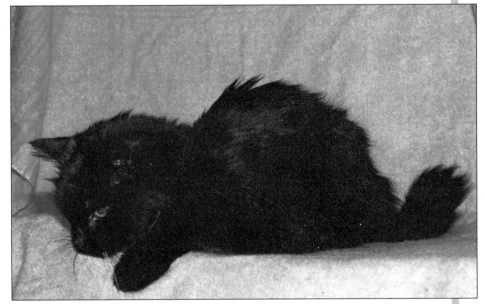

Signs of aging will eventually begin to show in even the most cared-for cat (*above*). They may include muscle wasting, increased thirst, general lethargy, and gradual diminishing of the senses especially eyesight and hearing. Regular veterinary check-ups are advisable to try and treat any disease problems, slow down any deterioration, and insure that your pet is not in pain.

DISEASES OF OLD AGE

Age makes an old cat vulnerable to many diseases that a younger animal can shrug off and there are a number of veterinary problems that are special to the elderly cat.

There are several disease problems that can occur in elderly cats, and owners should be on their guard for signs of them. It is always wise to turn to your veterinarian for advice as soon as you notice a problem — the use of home or pet shop remedies can be harmful and will probably allow the condition to become more firmly entrenched before effective treatment is started.

WEIGHT LOSS AND INCREASED THIRST

It is very common for elderly cats to lose weight gradually and drink more fluids. This may be a part of your cat's natural aging process, but could be due to a specific disease that requires treatment. Regular veterinary checks every six or nine months are a good idea for your cat anyway, but if you notice a fairly sudden increase in drinking or a severe loss of weight, you should have your cat checked without delay. It is a good idea to weigh elderly cats every two or three months and keep a note of their weight so that you will know if they are losing or gaining — it can be very difficult to detect changes by sight alone if you are seeing the cat every day. There are four common causes of weight loss and increased thirst in older cats.

Kidney disease — The best known, and probably the most common, is *chronic interstitial nephritis*, a form of kidney disease. If your veterinarian suspects this disease, he may take a blood test to measure your cat's *blood urea* levels. This is the best test for measuring whether a cat is suffering from some degree of kidney failure. Cats with kidney disease will also tend not to eat, have bad breath, and may suffer from vomiting and/or diarrhea. It is

important to realize that by the time signs of this disease develop in an elderly cat with kidney failure, a large part of both kidneys will have been irreversibly damaged and replaced with scar tissue. Therefore, any treatment that your veterinarian gives can only prevent further deterioration — kidney transplants are still a long way off for cats! Treatment for kidney disease may include an attempt to increase the amount of starchy foods the cat eats, (see p. 42) but this may not be successful with a cat that is not eating well anyway. It is better for the cat to eat anything rather than nothing at all. Your veterinarian may well prescribe drugs to try to support your cat. These often include *anabolic steroids*, which help to build up body weight and slow down muscle wasting. Under the guidance of your veterinarian, you should also administer a suitable vitamin supplement, since cats tend to lose certain vitamins through the kidneys when they are not functioning normally. While some cats do not respond at all well to treatment for kidney disease, there are many cats that do seem to respond and, with treatment, have been able to live out a year or two of happy lives.

Diabetes — *Diabetes mellitus*, or sugar diabetes, is another less common cause of increased thirst. Cats with this disease are often overweight at first but then lose weight as the condition progresses. Sometimes it is possible to detect a smell of ketones, a smell like nail polish remover, on the breath of a diabetic cat. The condition can be diagnosed either by a urine or a blood test, a test that should not be

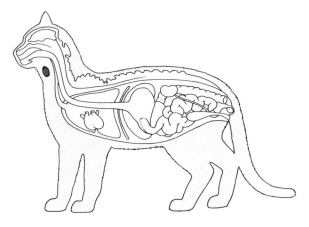

The thyroid gland is positioned in the neck (*above*), just below the angle of the jaw. When it is over-active, an enlargement can usually be felt in this region.

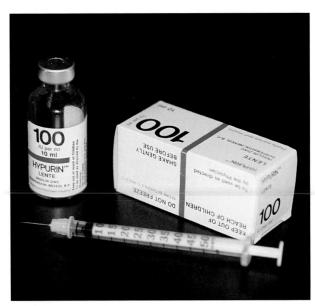

Diabetic cats may show some similar symptoms to hyperthyroid cats. They have to be trained to perform in a litter tray with only a little paper in it, so that the urine can be tested regularly. A small dose of insulin (*above*) has to be injected by the owner each day. Insulin that has been produced for human diabetics is also used to treat cats.

Over-activity of the thyroid speeds up the metabolism, so that affected cats (*above*) become very hungry, very thirsty, but lose weight and may develop chronic diarrhea. This cat had a very obvious enlargement in the neck region and a blood test demonstrated markedly elevated thyroid hormone levels.

carried out following a large meal. Treatment may involve a change of diet together with regular injections of insulin. The owner will probably have to collect a urine sample to test regularly. While most owners learn to cope with giving regular injections, they will also need to give a diabetic cat very regular care and attention for the rest of its life. Although the treatment of a cat with diabetes is not simple, many owners have enabled their diabetic cats to live out the final year or two of their lives in a reasonably normal and contented manner.

Overactive thyroid — More recently, *hyperthyroidism* has been discovered to be a fairly common cause of increased thirst and loss of weight in elderly cats. The disease is due to a growth in the thyroid gland in the neck. This growth is usually not cancerous, but it produces an excessive quantity of thyroid hormone. Affected cats usually have a voracious appetite, often with diarrhea, and may be hyperactive and nervous. It may be possible to feel a lump in the neck region; a blood test will confirm the diagnosis. While drugs can be used to control the problem, surgery provides the only cure, and although surgery on the thyroid glands is not without problems, many cats have now been successfully cured of this problem.

Cancer — *Neoplasia*, or cancer, is unfortunately fairly common in cats of all ages. It may affect any part of the body, and may lend itself well to surgical removal. The most common form in cats is *lymphosarcoma*, a cancer of the white blood cells, which may develop as a result of exposure to feline leukemia virus. This is discussed in more detail in Chapter 4. It is mentioned here as it is a common cause of weight loss in older cats, often despite a voracious appetite. In older cats it usually settles in the lymph nodes of the intestines or along the wall of the bowel, interfering with the absorption of food. If it affects the liver or kidneys, it may also cause increased thirst. Definitive diagnosis may be possible from the clinical signs or from a blood test, but it may be necessary to carry out an exploratory operation to remove a small piece of tissue for examination under the microscope. Anti-cancer drugs may be used to treat some mild cases of lymphosarcoma, but they will only prolong life and not cure the underlying problem. Other forms of cancer may affect the skin or any of the internal organs. Cancer is not one disease, but many different diseases that all result in excessive and uncontrolled growth of certain body tissues. Treatment will depend upon the type of tumor involved — it can include surgery, chemotherapy (drugs), or even radiotherapy.

HEART PROBLEMS

While cats do not get thickening of the arteries and coronary heart diseases as humans do, elderly cats are prone to *cardiomyopathy*, a degeneration of the heart muscle. This causes a build-up of fluid on the chest leading to labored breathing; it can also cause blood clots to form in the arteries. The most likely place for such clots to form is in the arteries supplying the legs. This causes *iliac thrombosis* and results in severe cramps in the hind leg muscles. The outlook for cats with such symptoms is poor, since the underlying heart problem will remain even if the blood clot is removed surgically. Some cats with cardiomyopathy are treated with aspirin to discourage blood clotting, but since the drug can be very poisonous to cats, it must be given in very low doses under close veterinary supervision. Drugs may also be given to assist the heart and remove fluid from the chest, but unfortunately few cats survive with a weak heart.

OTHER PROBLEMS

Constipation — Occasionally, elderly cats develop a "lazy bowel," resulting in bouts of constipation. Some owners become very concerned if their cat does not have a bowel movement every day, but there is generally no need to worry unless your cat is straining and unable to move its bowels or has not moved them for several days. Do not confuse straining due to constipation with straining due to a urinary obstruction — the latter is a serious problem and requires immediate veterinary attention (see Chapter 4 for further details). If your cat does suffer from constipation, give a teaspoonful of mineral oil daily for a few days — if the cat does not have a bowel movement within 24 hours or if it becomes distressed, contact your veterinarian. Frequent dosing with mineral oil may affect the absorption of certain vitamins, and a balanced vitamin supplement should be given to compensate. Constipation can be aggravated if the

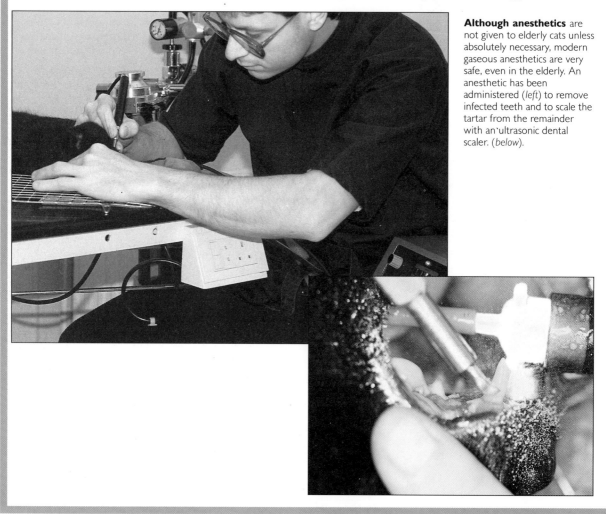

Although anesthetics are not given to elderly cats unless absolutely necessary, modern gaseous anesthetics are very safe, even in the elderly. An anesthetic has been administered (*left*) to remove infected teeth and to scale the tartar from the remainder with an ultrasonic dental scaler. (*below*).

cat swallows a lot of hair. Regular grooming will help to prevent this. Examine the coat for signs of any problems that might be causing excessive molting, particularly fleas.

Incontinence — Some cats that have been housetrained throughout their lives may become *incontinent* when they get older. This may simply be due to laziness, and the cat may respond to more litter boxes around the house for it to use, and to retraining as discussed in Chapter 4. Unfortunately, some cats will still soil indoors. They should be checked by a veterinarian to see whether there is any physical problem, such as a urinary or kidney infection. If the cause is simply senility, the cat has either to be confined to an area where the soiling does not matter, or put to sleep.

Cataracts — Cloudiness of the lens within the eye is very common in the eyes of elderly cats. They usually progress gradually and do not cause blindness until they are well advanced. Elderly cats seem to adapt to a gradual loss of vision reasonably well, and although surgery to remove the cataracts is theoretically possible, it is not usually considered wise for an old cat.

Bad teeth — Due to an accumulation of tartar on the teeth over the years bad teeth are very common in older cats. Tartar will cause the gums to become inflamed (*gingivitis*) and to recede. This allows infection to attack the roots of the teeth (*periodontitis*), causing them to loosen and eventually drop out. Since this is painful for the cat, having the tartar removed before the gums become too inflamed will save a lot of discomfort later on. Naturally, the tartar will begin to accumulate again once the teeth have been cleaned — a diet that exercises the teeth may help to slow down the rate at which it builds up again. A small amount of dry cat food will exercise the teeth. Or your cat may like to chew on some gristle, such as the edge of a piece of steak.

INFLAMMATION OF THE GUMS

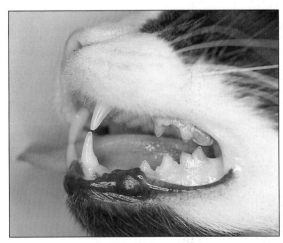
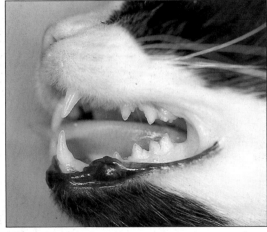

Tartar is formed on the teeth from an accumulation of food, bacteria, and substances in the saliva (*above, left*). Small amounts only discolor the teeth and possibly cause bad breath, but as it builds up it pushes on the gums and causes them to become inflamed, a condition known as *gingivitis*. If left untreated, the roots become infected, and the teeth become loose and painful. Removing the tartar by scaling the teeth under anesthetic "stops the rot" and allows the gums to heal (*above, right*). However, this does not prevent the further buildup of tartar with time, and regular scaling may be necessary. Even given identical diets, some cats seem to build up tartar more quickly than others, and there is probably a hereditary factor involved, associated with the composition of saliva.

EUTHANASIA

Since the cat may well have been a much loved member of the family, it is not surprising that many owners go through a very real period of mourning when the cat dies. The decision to have a cat put to sleep may be inevitable.

? HOW DO I KNOW IF MY CAT OUGHT TO BE PUT TO SLEEP?

Most veterinarians and cat owners would agree that it is not the length of a cat's life that is of prime concern, but the quality of its life. There is obviously no necessity to put down all cats at a certain age because they are old — different cats will age at different rates. There are plenty of sixteen-year-old cats around that still behave like kittens. Similarly, there is no need to put a cat to sleep simply because a terminal condition such as cancer has been diagnosed — the cat may well be able to live several more happy months before life becomes a misery. If your cat is very old or unwell, you must decide whether he or she is still getting any enjoyment out of life or whether you are just prolonging life to avoid having to make a difficult decision or because you cannot bear to part with your pet. Do not be afraid to discuss the matter with your veterinarian. He or she will be happy to offer advice — but remember, you are the person living with your cat, you are in the best position to judge the quality of life your cat is having and only you can make the final decision when the time comes.

It may be necessary to put a cat to sleep that has a severe behavioral problem, such as severe incontinence, that makes it unsuitable as a pet. There is a limit to the inconvenience that any owner can be expected to tolerate, particularly if the cat is posing a health hazard. It is not wise to re-home a cat with behavioral problems unless the new owner is fully aware of the nature of the problem and is confident of being able to cope.

An even more difficult decision may have to be made if the owner of a cat is no longer able to keep a pet, perhaps due to a change of accommodation or moving overseas. It can be very difficult to re-home an adult cat, and many older cats do not adapt at all well to a change of home. Euthanasia may be the only alternative, but it is always unpleasant to have to put a healthy animal to sleep.

? HOW CAN I TELL IF MY CAT IS IN PAIN?

It is impossible to measure what pain any animal is feeling when unwell — we can only look at the nature of its disease and the way the animal is behaving and make a subjective judgment of what it must be feeling. A cat may make obvious signs, such as growling or screaming when certain parts of its body are touched, to show that it is in pain. Or it may display symptoms that must be unpleasant for it, such as repeated vomiting. In fact, cats generally seem to be most tolerant to what we would consider to be painful stimuli by producing natural painkillers known as *endorphins* in the brain. Many owners do not realize that their cats are ill until the disease is very advanced because cats

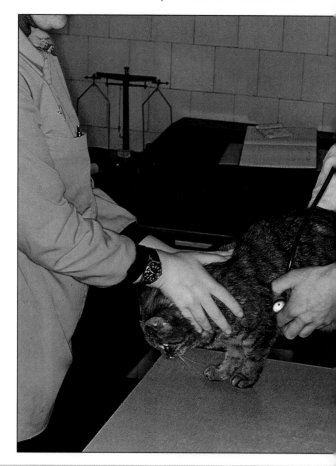

are so good at masking their illnesses and coping with life as best as possible.

As an owner, you will be familiar with the normal behavior pattern of your cat and will soon notice if there is a change. If your cat is eating normally, seems alert, and is going about life as usual, you can reasonably assume that it is not in any great degree of pain. If you are in doubt, do not hesitate to discuss the matter with your veterinarian.

 IS IT KINDER TO LET MY CAT DIE NATURALLY OR TO HAVE HIM PUT TO SLEEP?

Many owners dread having to make a decision to put their pet to sleep, and when that pet is very old or terminally ill, they naturally hope that the cat will die peacefully in its sleep. This would be fine if one could be sure that the end would be painless and peaceful, but unfortunately that is often not the case. In that sense, our pets are lucky — it is not necessary for them to suffer when the time comes for them to end their days. Euthanasia is quick and painless and need cause the cat no more pain or

If a terminal disease is proved to be painful and the need for medication becomes a constant necessity — when happiness turns to misery — it is time to put the cat to sleep.

distress than having an anesthetic. It is usually kinder to find the courage to make a decision and insure that your cat is put quickly and painlessly to sleep than to risk the possibility of a drawn out and painful death.

 SHOULD I HAVE MY CAT PUT TO SLEEP AT HOME?

Since a visit to the veterinarian's office can be a frightening experience for cats, many owners want their cat to end its days in its own environment at home. However, many veterinarians feel that the procedure can be carried out more quickly and painlessly in their offices. Since a house visit will take up very much more of your veterinarian's time, it will also be considerably more expensive than taking the cat to the office. Discuss the matter with your veterinarian; he will advise you depending on the nature of your cat and his personal opinion on the issue.

 HOW DOES A VET PUT A CAT TO SLEEP?

Pet cats are normally put to sleep with an injection of a large dose of a barbiturate, either into a vein of a leg or directly into an organ such as a kidney. The drug usually works very quickly, with the cat becoming unconscious within seconds and its breathing and heartbeat stopping soon afterwards. The drug used is very similar to that used for anesthesia and causes no pain other than the pinprick caused by the needle itself. If the cat is very difficult to handle, it may be necessary for the veterinarian to administer a sedative first, or to put the cat into a chamber into which an anesthetic gas can be administered. While this is not as quick as a barbiturate injection, it may be kinder for a cat that is very frightened of being handled.

 WHAT ARRANGEMENTS SHOULD I MAKE FOR MY CAT AFTERWARD?

Most owners leave the arrangements to the veterinarian who has put the cat to sleep. Pet animals are usually collected from the office and cremated, or buried at a landfill site. If you wish your cat to be buried in a pet cemetery or individually cremated, your veterinarian should be able to arrange it on your behalf. Some owners prefer to bury their pets in their own yard — that is fine if you have a suitable site, but be sure that you bury the cat at least three feet deep, preferably placing a paving stone over the site afterward to prevent the grave being dug up by scavengers such as foxes.

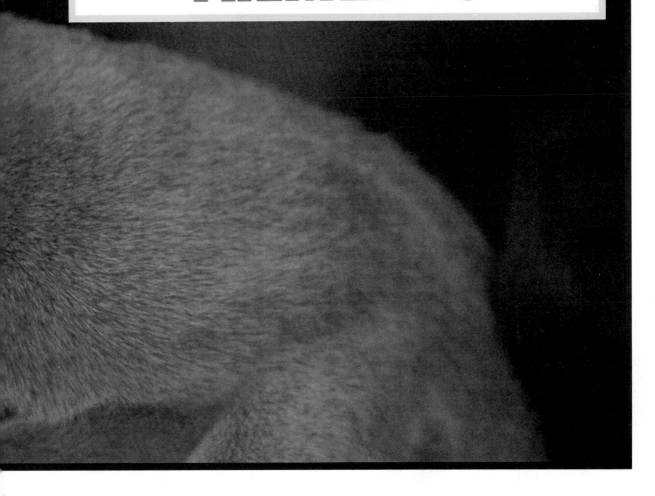

SECTION 2
UNDERSTANDING YOUR CAT'S AILMENTS

GENERAL MEDICAL CARE

4

It is helpful to be able to recognize some of the common problems that your cat may develop and an observant owner is a great asset in the detection of the early stages of an illness. The owner of a cat can provide many clues that help the veterinarian make the correct diagnosis, which in turn helps the cat make a speedy recovery. Understanding the causes of the more common ailments and problems that may afflict a cat helps the owner appreciate the importance of any treatment or nursing that may have to be continued at home.

Modern surgery and nursing techniques enable the most complex and sophisticated veterinary treatment to be carried out successfully (*right*).

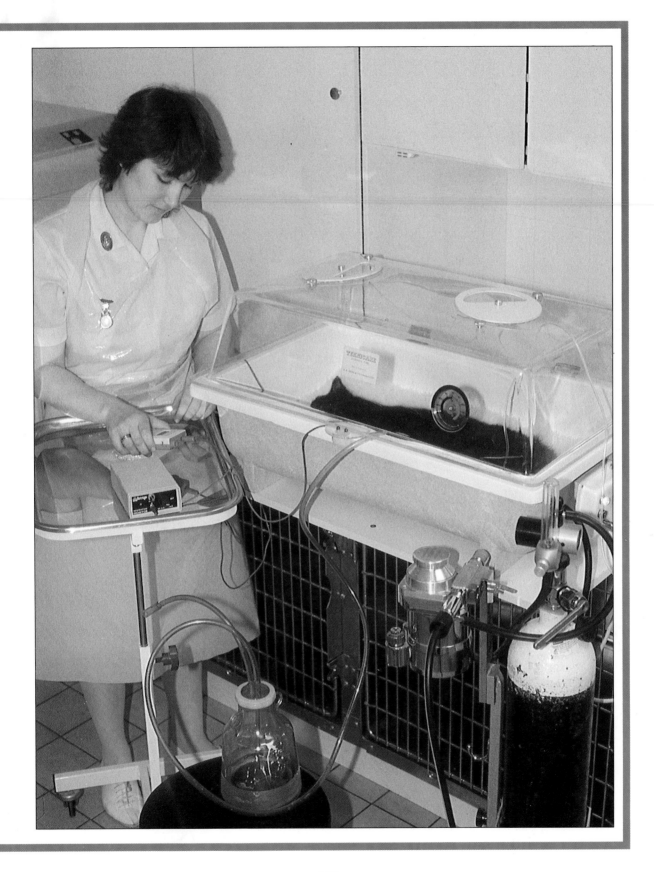

103

YOUR VET

Choosing a vet in whom you feel able to place confidence, is very important. A consultation will help you to understand and alleviate the root cause of your cat's illness and so will benefit your cat.

HOW CAN I CHOOSE A VETERINARIAN?

Lists of veterinarians can be found in the Yellow Pages of the local telephone directory, but if you do not already know a veterinarian in your area, it is best to ask friends with pets or local cat breeders to recommend someone for you. The office closest to you may not necessarily be the best for you, but remember that you may need to get to the office quickly in an emergency. Most pet owners are looking primarily for a veterinarian whom they feel genuinely cares about their pet and its problems, and they want to have confidence in his or her professional skills and the facilities that are available to back them up. A lot will therefore depend on the "chemistry" of your relationship with the veterinarian concerned, but on your first visit to the office you should gain an impression of the cleanliness of the public areas and the friendliness and efficiency of the nursing staff, as well as of your new veterinarian. A large multi-vet practice may be able to offer more elaborate facilities than a single-handed practice, but you may find a larger practice more impersonal. If you do decide to attend a multi-vet practice, find out whether you can arrange to see the same veterinarian each time for routine problems. Do not be afraid to ask about the facilities that are available at the office, whether the practice is prepared to make house calls if necessary, and about emergency services — every practice should offer a 24 hour service to its clients for urgent cases. The fees charged may well relate to the standard of facilities offered — every

veterinarian has to charge a consultation fee for his time, not only to cover his own income, but to pay for the ancillary staff, the capital invested in buildings and equipment, and the day to day overhead expenses such as heating, electricity, taxes, vehicle expenses and disposable items used. While the fee for a five or ten minute consultation with the veterinarian may seem high, only a small proportion of that amount actually goes to pay the salary of the veterinarian himself. While it should therefore be obvious that it is unwise to select a veterinarian on the basis of the fees charged alone, it does not necessarily follow that the most expensive practice in your area will be the best equipped — you must make a judgment as to which practice appears to offer the best service for the level of fees charged.

IS IT BETTER TO GO TO A VETERINARIAN WHO RUNS AN APPOINTMENT SYSTEM?

It is a matter of personal preference. Having an appointment system rather than an open office during certain hours means that the veterinarian can spread out his workload so that he does not have a

sudden rush of patients all at one time. This means that you may not have to wait as long to see the veterinarian and that your cat is less likely to have to mix with other sick pets in the waiting room. However, you may prefer the spontaneity of being able to pick up your pet and take it down to the office on the spur of the moment. If you do attend an office with an appointment system, you should confirm that they are willing to fit in urgent cases at short notice if necessary.

DO I NEED TO REGISTER WITH THE VET?

Contact the vet's office when you take on a new pet and find out if they prefer to take down your details before you first need to visit — it is not usually necessary but will provide a good opportunity to find out about office hours, vaccination policy, and to ask any other questions you may have. It is certainly a good idea to get to know your veterinarian before an emergency arises if possible — the relaxed atmosphere of a routine visit to administer vaccinations and give a health examination is an ideal opportunity to get to know your new veterinarian

and to discuss any general queries you may have about the care of your pet. Familiarity with your veterinarian may benefit your cat.

? HOW SHOULD I GET MY CAT TO THE VET'S OFFICE?

It is important that you transport your cat or kitten in a suitable cat box or basket, or at the very least, in a sturdy closed cardboard box with ventilation holes (see Chapter 1 for details of the types of cat baskets and boxes available). Even though you may feel confident that you can hold on to your cat firmly to prevent escape, havoc can break out in a waiting room when a Great Dane decides that your pet looks like a rather tasty snack!

? IS IT ALL RIGHT TO SEND SOMEONE ELSE WITH MY CAT TO THE VET IF I AM UNABLE TO ATTEND MYSELF?

For the veterinarian to be able to do his or her job properly, he or she needs to be able to obtain a lot of information about the cat and its problem. The task will be made much more difficult if you send the cat with someone who does not know very much about the cat.

The consulting room where the initial examination is carried out (*above*). As with all areas where sick animals are taken, all surfaces should be easily cleanable to prevent cross-infection, and free of unnecessary clutter.

The reception staff will be friendly and helpful (*left*). They should be able to offer advice on routine care of your pet, and help to iron out any queries you may have.

Most practices will have extensive back-up facilities — a laboratory and X-ray equipment — available behind the scenes to assist with diagnosis and treatment (*right*).

❓ WHAT SHOULD I DO IF I CANNOT AFFORD VETERINARY FEES?

Keeping a pet is a luxury rather than a necessity, and before you take a cat on, you should consider whether you are likely to be able to cope with the financial responsibilities involved. Naturally, circumstances may change or a sudden unexpected illness or accident may leave the owner of a cat faced with a large bill that he or she is unable to meet. The most important advice is to discuss the problem with your veterinarian at the outset — he may be able to arrange for you to stagger your payments over a period of time or to take your cat to one of the animal charities' clinics that exist to help owners genuinely unable to afford veterinary fees. While most of these clinics used to be poorly equipped and poorly staffed, and some still are, many of them are now very modern and well equipped and are able to deal with even the most complicated of cases. Please remember that these facilities are provided entirely by voluntary donations — do not use them unless you are genuinely unable to pay for private veterinary fees because you may well deprive another pet owner who really does need help. If you are unable to manage, simply make a donation..

❓ IS PET INSURANCE WORTHWHILE FOR MY CAT?

There are several insurance companies in the United States offering insurance against veterinary fees incurred. Most veterinarians keep a supply of proposal forms in their waiting rooms for their clients, and are happy to offer advice on pet insurance in general. It is wise to look at the cover provided by several companies — the price and the degree of protection offered may differ between policies, and some companies may offer insurance cover for cats at a lower premium than that for dogs. Of course, the insurance companies can only make a living if the value of overall claims is less than the total premiums paid, but on an individual basis, pet insurance does offer cat owners the assurance that they are not going to have to pay a large bill unexpectedly and that any necessary treatment can be carried out regardless of the costs involved.

❓ WHAT SHOULD I DO IF I AM UNHAPPY WITH THE SERVICE OR TREATMENT PROVIDED BY MY VETERINARIAN?

If you decide to change to another veterinarian because you are unhappy with the services provided by your present one, and if your cat has not recently received any treatment, there is no problem. You are free to choose to take your business where you please. A problem can arise if your cat is receiving treatment and you become unhappy about the diagnosis or treatment and feel that you would like a second opinion. You are entitled to a second opinion but it is pointless to turn up at another vet's office and expect the treatment to be continued there. No veterinarian is permitted ethically to take over a case from a colleague without having contacted the first vet to obtain a full case history of tests carried out and treatment given and gained his permission to take over the case. Apart from being a professional courtesy, this procedure is vital to insure that tests already carried out are not repeated unnecessarily and that treatment is not given that would conflict with drugs previously administered. If you are worried about the treatment that your cat is receiving, it is best to be frank with your veterinarian and politely explain your concern to him. You will probably find him very willing to arrange a second opinion for you, probably with a veterinarian who has a particular interest and knowledge of the type of problem that your cat is suffering from.

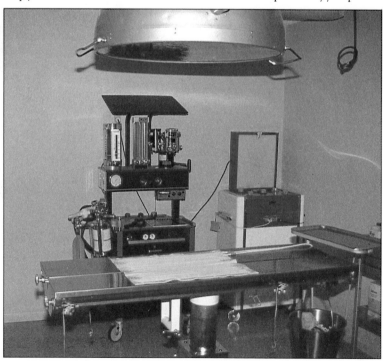

Surgical operations can be carried out at most practices when necessary. The surgical facilities and the standard of equipment are comparable to the facilities available in human hospitals, including areas for general treatment, surgical preparation, instrument sterilization, an operating theater (*left*) and hospitalization facilities. Many practices are happy to arrange a tour of their inpatient areas on request.

GENERAL NURSING

Some useful hints to help you care for your sick cat. Simply knowing how to pick up a cat, weigh it or tempt it to take food can make nursing and looking after your pet much easier for you.

? WHAT IS THE NORMAL BODY TEMPERATURE OF A CAT?

The normal temperature is considered to be 101.5°F, but this is an average figure, and there can be a fair amount of variation even in perfectly heathy cats. The temperature is taken with a thermometer inserted carefully into the rectum. This is not always an easy procedure with a cat, and it is best carried out by experienced veterinary or nursing staff.

? HOW CAN I WEIGH MY CAT?

Pick up your cat and weigh yourself holding the cat on bathroom scales. Then weigh yourself alone and deduct the difference. Alternatively, you can put the cat on scales in a cat box and then deduct the weight of the empty box. It's easy when you know how!

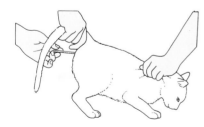

The temperature of a cat is usually taken rectally with a well-lubricated thermometer (*above*). However, it is not a procedure that is taken to kindly by most cats, and is probably best left to the veterinarian.

? WHAT IS THE CORRECT WAY TO HANDLE A CAT?

A placid cat can be picked up with one hand supporting the chest and the other under the rump — it can then be cradled in the arms. If the cat is fractious, grasp the scruff firmly in one hand and help support its weight by holding the hind feet with the other hand.

? HOW CAN I TEMPT A SICK CAT TO EAT?

Cats prefer to eat food that is at body temperature — presumably a throw-back to their natural instinct to eat freshly killed meat. Therefore, it is best to warm food slightly before presenting it to a sick cat. They are also loath to eat food if they are unable to smell it first. This is a particular problem in cats with cat 'flu because the nose is blocked and they are unable to use their sense of smell. Cats with 'flu may also have sore mouths, and a soft diet will be easier for them to manage. The exact type of food to offer depends very much on what your cat's preferences are, but mashed up pilchards in plenty of oil is a favorite with many. For the very sick cat, you could try a liquified meat extract.

? HOW LONG CAN A CAT SURVIVE WITHOUT EATING?

Quite a long time — probably at least two or three weeks, depending on how much reserve the cat had before the fast began. However, dehydration can kill very rapidly, particularly if the cat is losing fluids due to diarrhea or vomiting. Therefore, getting fluids into a sick cat is more urgent than persuading the cat to eat. If the cat is unable to keep down sufficient quantities of fluid or cannot be persuaded to take in fluids, the veterinarian may have to administer saline by means of a drip, either into a vein or under the skin.

PICKING UP A CAT

A placid cat will generally feel more comfortable if cradled in the arms, (*above, left*), with the lower hand either supporting the cat's weight under its rump, or holding onto the legs. A more nervous or aggressive cat (*above, right*) should be restrained firmly by its scruff, with one hand, and the other hand again, either supporting its rump or holding the legs.

SIGNS OF GOOD HEALTH

? HOW CAN I TELL IF MY CAT IS UNWELL?

Cats are creatures of habit, and you will soon become familiar with the normal behavior pattern of your own cat. Any sudden change may be an early indication that trouble is brewing. For example, while most owners are not aware of how much water their cat drinks they will often notice if the cat starts to drink more than normal or, if a cat that has not drunk much at all suddenly starts drinking from the tap or the garden pond. Some of the external signs that give an indication of the cat's health include:

(1) **EYES** – They should be bright and alert but may become dull and sunken if the cat is ill. While some cats have a little "sleep" in the eyes occasionally, any soreness of the eyes or heavy discharge should receive veterinary attention. The third eyelids will sometimes cover the corner of the eyes if the cat is unwell

(2) **EARS** – It should not be necessary to clean the ears of a healthy cat. Any discharge or irritation may be a sign of an ear problem.

(3) **NOSE** – A discharge from one or both nostrils should not be ignored, particularly if it is thick and yellow. If the skin on the tip of the nose loses its normal pink color, the cat may be anemic or in shock.

(4) **MOUTH** – The teeth may have a heavy build up of tartar – this will require treatment if it is inflaming the gums. Ulcers within the mouth are common in cases of cat flu. Bad breath may be a sign of oral disease or kidney problems.

(5) **SKIN** – This should be free of parasites, and elastic and loose over the body – if the cat is dehydrated, the skin will lose its elasticity and stay in a "tent" when lifted from the body. The coat, which should normally be smooth and glossy in a short-haired cat, may become fluffed up or "spiky."

(6) **ANUS** – If the cat has diarrhea the anus may be soiled or sore.

• **Breathing** – If the cat is suffering from a chest problem breathing may be rapid and labored – sometimes the cat appears to be breathing with the abdominal muscles rather than with the chest alone.

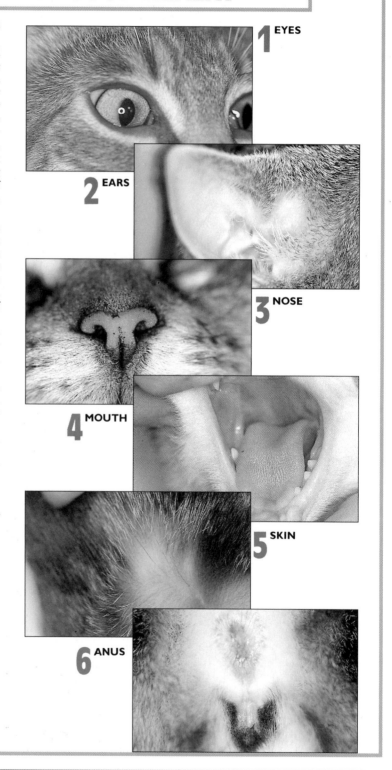

1 EYES

2 EARS

3 NOSE

4 MOUTH

5 SKIN

6 ANUS

HOW CAN I FORCE-FEED A SICK CAT?

The ease with which you are able to carry out force-feeding will depend very much on the nature of the cat concerned – it is impossible in some cases. Do not administer food or fluids too quickly, or the cat will be unable to swallow and they go down the windpipe into the chest where they can cause serious pneumonia. Food has to be administered in a liquidized form, and your veterinarian will be able to provide you with a syringe with which to administer it. The head should be held firmly upward and the food or fluids slowly dribbled into the mouth, pausing for the cat to swallow. Some cats will tolerate this fairly well, and the feeding may be invaluable in keeping up its strength. But other cats resent it violently, and you may do more harm than good if you have to use too much force.

If you are unable to force-feed your cat, and the lack of food and fluids is becoming critical, your veterinarian may decide to carry out a *pharyngostomy* operation to place a tube into the stomach from the side of the neck so that foods can be introduced through the tube. This is surprisingly well tolerated by most cats and can be continued over a period of several weeks if necessary. But the cat will probably have to be hospitalized while the tube is in place.

MY VET ASKED ME TO COLLECT A URINE SAMPLE FROM MY CAT – WAS HE JOKING?

Probably not, but he might not have been very optimistic that you would succeed! The first step is getting your cat used to using a litter box if it is not in the habit already; then substitute newspaper for cat litter; and finally just a small amount of newspaper in a very clean litter box and keep the cat indoors until it has performed in the tray – an early morning sample is best, but beggars can't be choosers! The excess that has not been soaked up by the paper can then be transferred into a jar. Be sure that it has been very well cleaned out with hot water and that there are no traces of sugar left in the jar if it contained food previously. Your veterinarian will probably not need a very large sample but it should be as fresh as possible – keep it in the refrigerator or a similar cool place if you cannot take it to the vet's office immediately.

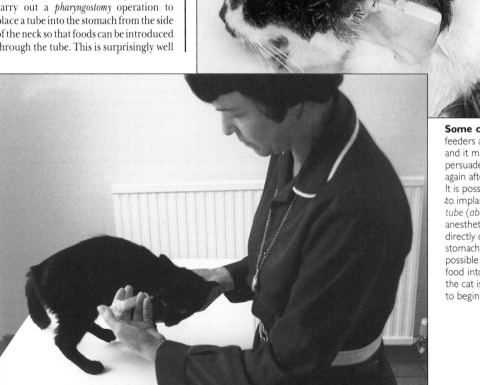

Some cats are very fickle feeders at the best of times, and it may be very difficult to persuade them to start to eat again after they have been ill. It is possible for a veterinarian to implant a *Pharyngostomy tube* (above) under general anesthetic from the throat directly down into the stomach. In this way it is possible to administer liquid food into the tube (*left*), until the cat is feeling well enough to begin eating again.

THE ELIZABETHAN COLLAR

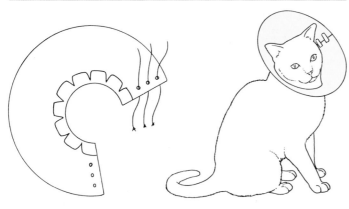

To prevent a cat from worrying a wound, an Elizabethan collar (*above*), made either from plastic or card, is sometimes used. Most cats find them quite an imposition, and it is probably best not to use one unless it is essential. Sedation may be necessary until the cat becomes accustomed to wearing the collar.

A protrusion of the third eyelid (*above*), a sign of a general illness rather than a disease of the eye itself. The eyelid normally sits tucked away in the inner corner of the eye and can be drawn quickly across the eye to protect it.

? WHAT DOES IT MEAN IF THE THIRD EYELID PROTRUDES OVER THE EYE?

This is a sign that the cat is unwell in some way, but it can be very non-specific. Some debilitated cats develop the problem, particularly if they have a heavy burden of worms. Or it may be due to a problem with the nerves that control the third eyelid — for example it can be a symptom of *feline dysautonomia* (see p.121), which is a very serious nervous disease and requires urgent attention. Or it can occur on its own with no other symptoms. In the latter case, it is probably due to a mild viral infection and will usually correct itself after two or three weeks without treatment, but a veterinary examination is nevertheless a good idea, to rule out any more serious problem. There is some controversy among veterinarians as to the cause and control of this "haws up" condition and the circumstances in which the third eyelid becomes prominent. It is a symptom of several disorders.

? WHAT CARE IS MY CAT LIKELY TO NEED AFTER AN OPERATION?

You should obtain information on feeding and aftercare from the veterinarian or animal healthy technician when you pick up your cat following surgery. The golden rule is that if you are unsure what to do, telephone the vet's office and ask. The office will not mind you calling for such information during normal working hours, or even out of hours if it is very urgent. Generally, cats should be fed a light diet in small amounts after an anesthetic. After some forms of bowel surgery, however, they may not be allowed to take food at all. It is vital to follow the directions you have been given in such cases, and to brief other members of the family also.

Any cat that has undergone surgery should be kept warm and under observation for at least 48 hours afterward. If you have other cats or dogs, be sure they do not pester the patient. Any appointments for re-examination at the vet's office must be strictly kept, and the wound checked regularly for any sign of undue swelling, pain, or discharge. Most cats will be sleepy for at least the first 24 hours after surgery, but if the patient does not seem to be slowly coming around, or improves but

GIVING A TABLET

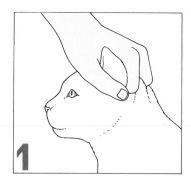

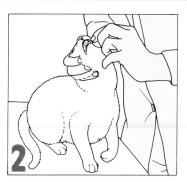

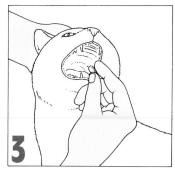

- Grasp the cat's head firmly on either side of the jaw (**1**).
- Bend the head gently but firmly backward until the lower jaw begins to drop open (**2**).
- Push the tablet onto the "V" right at the back of the cat's throat. It may go down more easily if it is lubricated with a bit of butter (**3**).

The cat should swallow immediately, but if it does not, keep the head held back and gently massage the throat to encourage it to swallow. Most cats will accept the administration of tablets in this way without anyone holding the rest of their bodies. Generally speaking the more you restrain the cat, the more it

will struggle. If, however, the cat keeps trying to scratch with its claws, it may be necessary to wrap the cat in a towel, so that only the head is sticking out.
- Drops can be administered in a similar way, but be careful to dribble them onto the tongue slowly. Otherwise, the cat may choke.

then becomes dull and refuses to eat, you should contact the veterinarian for advice. Cats are generally excellent surgical patients, and usually seem to recover from even the most major surgery remarkably quickly.

? WHAT IF MY CAT PULLS AT THE STITCHES?

Stitches are usually removed about seven to ten days following surgery, although this may vary. Sometimes dissolving stitches that do not have to be removed are used. Bandaging wounds is often not effective with cats, since they invariably see it as a challenge and go to great lengths to remove the wrapping! Cats will always lick at stitches and keep the wound clean — this does not usually do any harm, and there are substances in the saliva that may help to prevent infection. However, some cats take this too far and actually remove one or more of the stitches. If this is the case, and the wound is gaping open, veterinary advice should be sought without any delay. Sometimes a cat will be fitted with an Elizabethan collar to prevent the cat from doing any harm to the wound. Most cats are unhappy about such an imposition at first, but accept it within a day or two.

EAR AND EYE OINTMENTS

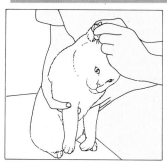

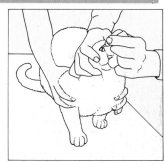

Ear drops
- Any dirt and wax should be gently cleaned from the ear before the drops·are applied.
- Hold the ear flap and use a cotton-tipped stick, but do not insert it deeper than the depth of cotton tip itself.
- Then, keeping hold of the ear flap firmly, allow the drops to drip into the ear canal — the cat may resent it less if you warm the bottle of drops in your hand first.
- Hold onto the ear flap long enough to allow the drops to run down deep into the ear.
- Clean away any excess ointment.

Eye drops
- Hold the head of the cat as if administering a tablet, but do not bend it backward.
- Approach with the bottle or tube from above, and either allow a drop to fall onto the surface of the eye, or pull the lower eyelid downward and put a small amount of ointment between the lower eyelid and the eye.
- Do not touch the surface of the eye with the bottle or tube, and do not allow the end of the bottle or tube to become contaminated.

VIRAL DISEASES

Intensive research into cats' illnesses in recent years has shown that many of the more common diseases that afflict cats are caused by viruses, the very smallest of living particles.

For many years cats were looked upon by veterinarians as strangely shaped dogs and treated as such. However, the increasing popularity of the cat as a pet has stimulated more study into feline medicine, and over the last 25 years vets have come to realize that the cat is in fact rather unique from the veterinary point of view, and great strides have been taken forward in our understanding of the diseases from which cats suffer.

The cat is unusual in that a large proportion of its disease problems are caused by viruses. Viruses are exceedingly small organisms that cannot reproduce themselves but invade the cells of the victim and cause the cells to manufacture more virus particles on their behalf. It is because viruses are so small and difficult to grow in the laboratory that the nature of so many feline diseases has remained a mystery for so long. This section of the book describes the important viruses that affect the cat. More details on transmission of viruses can be found on page 35.

FELINE PANLEUKOPENIA, also known as feline distemper, was the first disease of the cat that was proven to be caused by a virus (in 1964). The virus that causes the disease is very closely related to the *parvovirus* that has affected many dogs in recent years. It is similarly a very resistant virus that remains infective in the environment for many months and is difficult to kill with disinfectants. The main symptoms of feline distemper are severe vomiting and diarrhea, which develop two to ten days after exposure to the virus. Over half the cats that pick up the virus will probably die from it despite treatment. A pregnant female can infect her kittens while they are still in the womb, killing them or causing *cerebellar hypoplasia*, which affects the brain and makes the kittens uncoordinated and wobbly from the time of birth. Prompt treatment, particularly with intravenous fluids, may help to save some cases. Fortunately, a very effective vaccine is available against the disease and should be given regularly to all cats.

It is very difficult to rid a house of the virus once it has been contaminated — a 1 in 32 solution of bleach together with some dish-washing liquid is effective in killing the virus, but is not very pleasant for use in the household. If you should be unfortunate enough to have had a cat die from the disease, any cat introduced into the house over the following 12 months should have been vaccinated against the disease at least two weeks previously.

FELINE "CAT 'FLU" is a disease that can be caused by several different agents, but about 80 percent of cases are caused by one of the two feline respiratory viruses — *feline herpesvirus* (FVR) and *feline calicivirus* (FCI). Cats cannot catch influenza or cold viruses from humans. These two types of virus are much less resistant than the feline distemper virus, and, while they can be spread indirectly, they are usually spread by direct cat to cat contact or by aerosol inhalation due to sneezing. Each of the two types of virus tend to produce somewhat different symptoms which can develop as soon as 24 hours after infection. FVR causes the most severe form of feline respiratory disease, with runny eyes and nose and sneezing making the cat feel very unwell indeed. Some cats die due to dehydration or a secondary pneumonia. FCI may also cause runny eyes and nose, but typically results in the development of painful ulcers on the tongue, and sometimes on the mouth and nose.

Cat 'flu virus typically causes runny eyes, a runny nose, sneezing, a sore mouth, and a loss of appetite (*left*). It can be fatal, especially in young or weak cats, and most cases can be prevented by regular vaccination — it is too late to consider vaccination once your cat has contracted the disease. All kittens should be vaccinated and given annual booster injections.

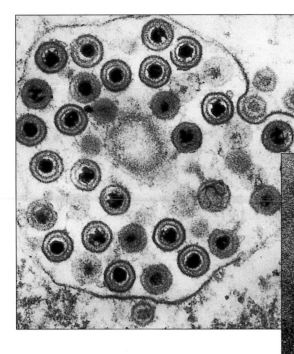

Feline *Herpesvirus*, is one of the causes of cat 'flu and this electron micrograph (*left*) shows its structural characteristics.

Coronavirus was recognized 20 years ago, as being the cause of feline infectious peritonitis (FIP). It is magnified 712,000 times by an electron microscope (*below*) and shown within a body cell.

At present there are no drugs that are effective in killing off the viruses once the cat has caught them, and treatment relies on antibiotics to prevent secondary infection, multivitamins to try to improve the cat's resistance, and careful nursing to keep the cat's strength up while it is trying to fight off the virus. Both viruses may linger in the nerve cells for many years, multiplying and causing bouts of illness when the cat is stressed and its defenses are lowered. The damage caused by the viruses may also leave the cat with a long-term conjunctivitis or runny nose (known descriptively as "chronic snuffles"). Vaccines are also available against these two major causes of feline respiratory disease and are widely used to prevent the disease. Eliminating the virus from the environment is not much of a problem since the viruses are susceptible to most common disinfectants or even to a dose of sunlight, but in multi-cat households it may be virtually impossible to identify and eliminate the cats that are carrying the viruses.

FELINE LEUKEMIA VIRUS (FeLV) is very common in cat populations and is probably the most common cause of death in adult cats, aside perhaps from the automobile. The virus cannot live for very long outside the body of its host, and transmission from cat to cat is by close contact, with the virus shed in the saliva in fairly large amounts. It is also possible for queens to infect their kittens in the womb before they are born. After infection with the virus, many cats will develop a resistance and simply expel it from their body. However, cats that are either very young when infected, or come into contact with a very large dose of the virus, are unable to rid themselves of the disease and become persistent carriers. The virus can go on to cause a wide range of diseases, including a cancer of the lymph tissue cells known as *lymphosarcoma*, (leukemia or cancer of the white blood cells) unfortunately a very common killer of cats of all ages. The virus may also cause damage to the bone marrow and chronic anemia or immunosuppression — a form of feline AIDS, in which the body is unable to defend itself against other infections. It should be stressed that humans cannot catch AIDS from cats.

FeLV is often suspected as an underlying cause of many non-specific illnesses and of infertility, and veterinarians will often carry out a blood test for the virus if they suspect FeLV could be playing a part in the problem. It is also common practice nowadays to give regular blood tests to cats that live in large groups, where the disease is most common. The owner of a pedigreed cat will often be asked to have his or her cat's blood tested before a visit to the stud tom. The stud tom should also have been regularly tested. This is a wise precaution since mating is an ideal opportunity for the virus to spread, and there is very little that can be done to treat FeLV infection once it has become established.

Some cats that show a positive result on the blood test are fighting off the virus and may not become carriers — cats that are positive on one test should be isolated and re-tested after 12 weeks. If the cat is unwell with the infection, or if it poses a risk to other cats in the household, it is probably best to put it to sleep. A vaccine against FeLV is available in the United States, but it is expensive and thought to protect fully only about 80 percent of the cats to whom it is given. It is hoped that cheaper and even more effective vaccines against FeLV will soon become available worldwide.

FELINE INFECTIOUS PERITONITIS (FIP) has been known in the cat world for many years, but the virus causing the disease was only identified in 1966. The virus cannot survive for very long outside the body and does not seem to be very

ANIMAL VECTORS OF RABIES

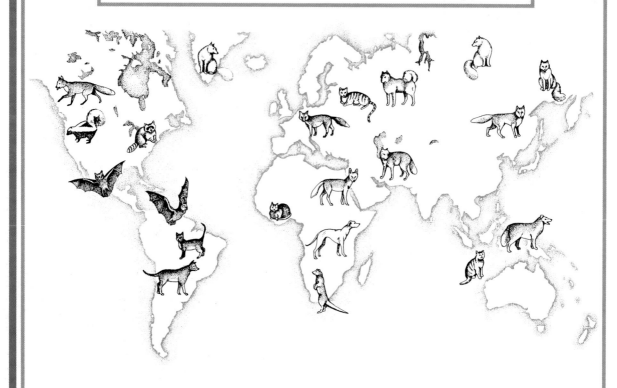

The distribution of rabies is world-wide and in places where the disease occurs regularly there is usually a "reservoir" of the infection in wild animals — foxes in Western Europe, skunks and raccoons in the United States, mongooses in South Africa, India and the Caribbean and vampire bats in Central and South America. Australia, the United Kingdom, Antarctica and Hawaii are the few rabies-free places in the world — thanks to their isolation by water and extremely strict import controls.

easily passed from cat to cat, but once a cat becomes infected, it usually goes on to develop FIP. The disease often starts with non-specific symptoms such as a lack of appetite and a high temperature, but the cat then goes on to develop an accumulation of fluid in the abdomen and sometimes on the chest. The abdomen becomes swollen, and breathing may become labored.

Examination of the fluid is often enough to confirm the diagnosis and, although a blood test is available, the results may be difficult to interpret. Some cats develop a different form of the disease (without the production of fluid) and have a wide range of symptoms due to the virus affecting the kidneys, liver, eyes, or nervous system. Diagnosis of these cases may be extremely difficult. Unfortunately, there is no effective treatment for the disease, and death is almost certain once symptoms develop. No vaccine is at present available as a preventative measure.

RABIES is one of the most feared of all diseases. The rabies virus can affect all warm-blooded species, including man. Although most people think the main risk to humans comes from the dog, in areas where rabies is established in the wildlife population a large percentage of human contacts with the disease come via the domestic cat. Infection usually occurs from a bite wound, with the virus intially multiplying in the wound and then traveling up a nerve to the brain. Although most animals develop symptoms about three weeks later, the incubation period may last for several months in rare cases.

There are two types of symptoms produced by the rabies virus: "dumb rabies" manifests itself primarily as muscle paralysis, and the cat may seem quieter and more friendly than normal; "furious rabies" is more usual in the cat, and, as the name suggests, it becomes wild and vicious, roaming over long distances to seek out victims to bite. In both types of the disease, the muscles responsible for swallowing become paralyzed, so that the animal is unable to eat or drink and drools saliva. While not all animals that are bitten by an affected animal develop the disease, once any symptoms begin to develop, death is inevitable.

SKIN DISORDERS

Parasites cause most of cats' skin problems and apart from ringworm, other skin disorders such as eczema, allergies, stud tail and balding are non-contagious and easily cleared.

? WHAT SORT OF SKIN PROBLEMS CAN FLEAS CAUSE MY CAT?

Some cats may have lots of fleas and not seem to mind, whereas other cats may be allergic to flea bites. Even one bite may result in a severe skin problem. Some cats may simply show signs of heavy molting and a dry, scurfy coat, whereas allergic cats may develop *miliary dermatitis*, which takes the form of small scabs, usually along the back. Continual licking by the cat will often wear away the hair and cause patches of baldness. Regular flea treatment is advisable and may be sufficient to control the problem. But if the skin is very raw, the cat may require antibiotics to clear any secondary infection, and possibly drugs to stop the irritation. Miliary dermatitis can be caused by an allergic reaction to other things, but fleas are by far the most common cause. Fleas can also infect the cat with tapeworm which uses the flea as

Some common external cat parasites are illustrated above:
Cheyletiella, fur mite (**1**).
Tombicula, harvest mite (**2**).
Felicola, cat louse (**3**).
Ixodes, sheep tick (**4**).
Ctenocephalides felis, cat flea (**5**).
Notoedres, head mange mite (**6**).

Fleas can produce a localized skin irritation by excessive licking and biting on one area. This may then become infected with bacteria, and cause a severe weeping of skin (*right*). Regular flea treatment is advisable for all cats, on the basis that prevention is better than cure.

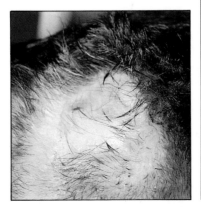

an intermediary host for its larvae. The larvae are swallowed with the carrier fleas when the cat grooms itself.

? WILL CAT FLEAS LIVE ON HUMANS?

No, but they'll have a lot of fun dying! The cat flea will not complete its life cycle in humans but will sometimes bite them.

OTHER EXTERNAL PARASITES

There are several other external parasites that can affect cats.

Ticks are blood-sucking, wingless insects that are occasionally picked up by cats in long grass. On farmland they usually come from sheep or cattle, but animals such as hedgehogs may carry them into domestic gardens. Ticks bury their heads into the cat's skin and, since they are fixed and do not move, can easily be mistaken for small cysts, although on close examination the legs can be seen close to the skin. Great care should be taken not to pull them off and leave the head in place. It is best to kill them first by spraying them directly with a veterinary flea spray — they will then shrivel up and drop off within 24 hours or they can then be pulled from the skin easily, complete with head. These animal ticks do not usually affect humans.

Lice are occasionally seen, mainly in kittens. The adult louse, another wingless insect, lays its eggs and attaches them to the hairs — the small white eggs are often visible and are called nits. The whole of the life cycle is therefore spent on the host, so that regular treatment of the cat itself should clear the problem. Infection can occur from cat to cat only by contact, although lice can be transmitted on shared grooming implements. They are very fussy about the species of host they choose and cannot affect human hair.

Ear mites are about the size of a small pinhead and live in and around the ears of cats. They are very common, especially in kittens, and cause the production of a large amount of black wax. Some cats do not seem to be very troubled by mites, while others find them very irritating, and their persistent scratching can cause a lot of inflammation and secondary infection. They are transmitted from cat to cat by close contact and cannot affect humans, although they can affect dogs, in which case they often cause even more irritation than with cats. Your veterinarian will be able to diagnose the problem by the nature of the wax and by looking in the ear with an auriscope to see the mites. He will prescribe ear drops to kill off the mites. It is important that all in-contact dogs and cats are treated at the same time, and that treatment is continued for three to four weeks to kill off the eggs of the mites as they hatch out.

Cheyletiella mites are sometimes called "walking dandruff mites" because they are small and white and just about visible to the naked eye; it looks as though the cat has dandruff moving on its back. These can be picked up from other affected cats, dogs or rabbits, and may cause a skin irritation and rash on the owner. They live on the surface of the skin, sometimes digging shallow tunnels into it, and attach their eggs to the hairs. Shampoo preparations must be used regularly to clear the problem.

Harvest mites are small orange or red mites that are just visible to the naked eye and sometimes cause irritation of the head, ears or legs, particularly in the fall. A flea spray will normally clear them.

Mange is very rare in cats in the United States, but can cause irritation and crusting of the skin. It may be due to either the *Notoedres cati* or the *Demodex cati* mite.

Maggots can cause a serious problem by invading the tissues of sick or debilitated cats. It is therefore important to keep infected wounds, especially around the anal region, clean and free of flies, especially in summer.

OTHER CAUSES OF SKIN DISORDERS

Although parasites cause a large proportion of skin problems in cats, there are many other possible causes. Some of the most important include:

Ringworm which, despite its name, is caused by a fungus that grows on the hairs – not by a worm. Ringworm is common in many species and can be transferred from one species to another, including man. The ringworm most commonly found is called *Microsporum canis*, and usually causes white, scaly, bald patches, especially around the head region. Some cats carry the fungus and show only mild symptoms

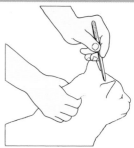

REMOVING A TICK

Ticks should never be pulled off the skin wile still alive, or the head may be left buried in the skin and cause a severe reaction. The best way to kill the tick is to spray it with a potent insecticide, such as is used for fleas, and to allow it time to die and subsequently drop off. Or, if necessary, pull it off with a pair of tweezers.

Hormonal alopecia results in the loss of hair on certain areas of the body (*left*), especially the lower abdomen and the flanks, due to a delayed growth of new hair. The skin is not itchy or sore, and the problem may be seasonal.

Ticks may vary in size and color, and bury their heads into the cat's skin so as to attach themselves firmly and to suck blood (*above*). In some tropical countries they may release poisons into the blood of the cat, causing *Tick paralysis*.

such as a somewhat scurfy coat. Cat ringworm can usually be seen to glow green under a special ultraviolet light known as a Wood's Lamp. It may also be visible on the hairs under a microscope. The most accurate form of diagnosis is to take a hair sample and try to grow the fungus in the laboratory, but this can take up to three weeks to produce a result.

The disease is not uncommon, and since the spores of the fungus are resistant to disinfectants and can stay in the environment for a long time remaining infectious, ridding the household of the fungus can be difficult. Certain medical preparations can be used for localized problems, but affected cats usually have to be treated with tablets of an antifungal drug called griseofulvin. This drug protects the cat by being incorporated into new hairs as they grow, so initial clipping of the hair followed by up to three months of treatment may be necessary.

Feline endocrine alopecia is a hormonal imbalance seen in neutered males and females. Bald patches of skin appear, usually on the stomach and flanks. This can look like miliary dermatitis as described on p.115, but the skin is not itchy and has no scabs — the bald areas appear because the hair fails to grow properly, not because the cat is continually licking and pulling it out. This can be a seasonal problem, and if it is severe, the cat may need hormone treatment to control it. This problem should not be confused with a thinning of the hair in front of the base of the ears, which is usually completely normal.

Neurodermatitis due to excessive licking and grooming of the coat by nervous cats, often in response to a specific source of stress, and again may resemble miliary dermatitis. However, affected cats may respond to attempts to minimize the stress or to treatment with tranquilizers. It is most common in Siamese, Burmese and Abyssinian breeds of cat.

Eosinophilic granulomas are thickened and ulcerated skin lesions. They are often seen on the upper lip and in such cases may be called *rodent ulcers*. They may be caused by excessive grooming by the cat, and therefore fleas may be a contributory factor. Care must be taken to see that these lesions are not confused with skin cancers. It may be necessary for your veterinarian to send a small skin sample off to a laboratory to be sure. Most cases respond well to medical treatment, but surgery is sometimes necessary. In cryosurgery, the affected area is frozen with a very cold probe. This procedure can be used as an alternative to ordinary "sharp" surgery in some cases. However, tablets are usually effective.

Feline acne is a thickening of the skin due to infection of the lower lip. It is probably caused by an overproduction of natural oils of the skin glands in that region. It may be possible to clear the problem with topical treatment applied to the skin, or antibiotics may be prescribed.

Stud tail is a baldness and thickening of the skin on the tail near its base. It is usually seen only in entire tom cats, and is due to large numbers of special skin glands that develop in the area. In some cases, the area may become infected and sore and should be cleaned regularly with a surgical scrub.

Rodent ulcers are deep skin sores on the upper lip (*above, left*). Their cause is not known, although they may be aggravated by continual licking of an initial skin irritation. Most cases respond quite rapidly to anti-inflammatory treatment, (*above, right*). However, if your cat does not respond rapidly to treatment, it may be necessary to take a small biopsy specimen from the lesion so that it can be examined under the microscope to rule out any other possible causes, such as skin cancer.

RESPIRATORY DISEASES

Serious diseases of the nose, throat and lungs often manifest themselves in obvious symptoms very late. Immediate attention from your veterinarian is almost always an urgent necessity.

These can be divided into Upper Respiratory Disease, affecting mainly the nose and upper air passages, and Lower Respiratory Disease, affecting the lungs.

UPPER RESPIRATORY DISEASE

The most important of these is cat 'flu, and the majority of cases are caused by one of the two feline respiratory viruses (see p. 112). There are, however, several other agents that may cause similar symptoms. The treatment for any type of cat 'flu is generally the same, and although antibiotics to control secondary infection and possibly multivitamins may both be helpful, careful nursing is of paramount importance (see p. 107).

Chronic rhinitis is a term used to describe an inflammation of the nasal passages that has become well established over a period of time. It may follow secondary bacterial infection after a bout of cat 'flu, or it could be due to fungal infection, a foreign body such as a piece of grass that has been inhaled, or a growth in the nose.

Diagnosis of the cause of "chronic snuffles" may involve the use of X-rays, blood tests, and a culture in the laboratory of the bacteria present in the discharge. Treatment will involve trying to clear the cause of the problem, together with drugs to help alleviate the symptoms. Unfortunately, once the lining of the nasal passages have been severely damaged, a complete cure is often impossible, and the cat and its owner have to learn to live with the problem.

Pharyngitis and laryngitis Cats can also suffer from bouts of *pharyngitis*, sore throats, causing discomfort when swallowing, and *laryngitis*, which may cause the cat to lose its voice, a source of great worry to some owners, and a source of great joy to others! Both conditions usually respond well to antibiotic treatment.

LOWER RESPIRATORY DISEASE

A cough is relatively uncommon in cats, and disease of the lower respiratory tract usually manifests itself in the form of *dyspnea*, or labored breathing. This may be accompanied by other symptoms such as the cat feeling unwell and being reluctant to eat or to exercise.

When cats do cough, it is usually due to disease of the trachea (windpipe) or the bronchii — the larger airways into the lungs.

Bronchial asthma, an allergic chest problem, can cause cats to cough, but the cause may also be an infection. Chronic coughing, rather like chronic rhinitis, can often be a difficult problem to cure completely, and treatment often has to be continued on a permanent basis to control the problem.

Lungworms may also cause a cough and are quite common in young cats, but only rarely do they cause serious disease. Diagnosis of lungworm infection relies upon examination of the cat's stool under the microscope to identify the larvae of the worm, and specific drugs effective against lungworm must be used for its treatment.

Dyspnea is generally a symptom of a fairly serious lung disease, especially since breathing in cats usually does not become labored until the underlying disease is well advanced. There are several possible causes, and the first step is usually to take an X-ray to establish whether there is 'fluid on the chest or whether any other possible cause of the breathing problem such as a growth is visible. If 'fluid is present, the veterinarian will probably wish to drain off a sample for analysis. Causes of an accumulation of 'fluid on the chest include a chest infection, feline infectious peritonitis (see p. 113), a tumor within the chest, or heart disease (see p. 96). If the cat has been involved in a road accident or similar incident, the veterinarian will be looking for signs of a rupture of the diaphragm, the muscular sheet that divides the chest from the abdomen. Some of the causes of labored breathing such as most growths within the chest and feline infectious peritonitis are incurable, and any of the other causes are likely to require intensive treatment.

LIFE CYCLE OF A LUNGWORM

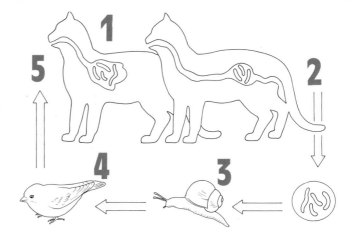

The adult lungworm lives in the lungs of cats (**1**). It lays eggs in the air passages, which are then coughed up and develop into larvae which are passed out in the motions (**2**). The eggs lie on the ground, until they are ingested by a molluscan intermediate host such as a snail (**3**). It is thought that these infected molluscs are then eaten by birds (**4**), which are then in turn eaten by cats (**5**).

CIRCULATORY DISEASES

Any disorder in the circulatory system — though heart trouble is relatively rare in cats — is potentially serious and many blood diseases need to be sampled for diagnosis. Anemia is a symptom.

HEART DISEASE

Heart disease is fortunately not very common in cats. They are spared from coronary thrombosis, which so often causes heart attacks in humans, and do not suffer from heart valve disease, a very common problem in older dogs. Plenty of **exercise may alleviate heart problems.**

Congenital heart disease covers a range of defects in the heart that are present at birth. These defects are very rare in cats — about 1 in 1000 kittens — and when they do occur may be mild and not cause any symptoms or illness. However, they may cause kittens to fail to thrive as they grow and if severe, usually necessitate the kitten being put to sleep.

Cardiomyopathy is the name given to a degeneration of the heart muscle, the only form of heart disease that is fairly common in the cat. It is a disease of old age and is discussed in more detail on page 96.

ANEMIA

Anemia is a reduction in the number of red blood cells circulating in the blood. It is not a disease itself but a sign of illness that can have many possible causes. The red blood cells are responsible for transporting oxygen in the blood; affected cats will tend to be breathless and lethargic. Since hemoglobin, the pigment in the red blood cells, gives the blood its red color, anemia will tend to make the cat "pale" — this is best seen by examining the membranes that line the eyes and mouth, the tongue, and the tip of the nose if it is not too heavily pigmented. This is another example of cats masking the signs of a problem very effectively until the disease is well advanced. If the cause of the anemia is not obvious from an examination of the patient, the veterinarian may have to carry out further tests before he can pinpoint the cause and treat it effectively. For example, he may carry out a blood test to measure the severity of the anemia, to see if the cat is making new red blood cells, and to gain any further clues as to the cause of the problem. It may even be necessary to take a sample of the bone marrow for examination — the diagnosis and treatment of anemia is very complex. Some of the important causes are:

Bleeding, either externally due to injury or blood-sucking skin parasites, or internally due to internal injuries, tumors, or disorders of the normal clotting mechanisms of the blood. Some rat poisons may cause the latter. In these cases a blood test will usually demonstrate that the cat is frantically trying to make new blood cells to compensate.

Bone marrow failure Red blood cells are manufactured in the bone marrow, which can be affected by many factors, including poisons and infections. The most likely causes of failure are infection with feline leukemia virus and chronic kidney failure. This type of anemia is very common, and unfortunately does not respond well to treatment.

Hemobartonella felis This single-celled parasite attaches to the red blood cells. These are then broken down by the cat's own defense mechanisms causing *feline infectious anemia.* It is not clear how the disease is transmitted from cat to cat — it is known that the blood is infective, and it is possible that a blood-sucking animal such as the flea could transmit it. The organism can usually be seen if the blood of an infected cat is examined under the microscope, but not always because sometimes the organisms can be found only intermittently in the blood of infected cats. The disease tends to be of a recurrent nature, with bouts of infection following periods of stress, and it is frequently associated with concurrent feline leukemia virus infection. It will usually respond well to treatment, although a long course of drugs may have to be given.

Anemia can be caused by one of many different diseases. It is often necessary for the veterinarian to take a blood test (*above*) to examine the blood to determine the cause of the problem. The blood is usually taken from the vein that runs along the front of the forearm, a procedure that generally causes very little pain or distress.

Iron deficiency anemia is less common in cats than it is in humans, but it may occur in kittens just before weaning because milk is quite low in iron. Since both iron and vitamin B_{12} are needed for the production of new blood cells, it is sensible to administer a vitamin and mineral supplement to cats that are recovering from anemia from any cause. Raw liver is also a rich source of iron and vitamins but should not be fed to excess.

The treatment of anemia should always commence with an attempt to identify and cure the underlying cause of the problem. Additional supportive treatment can be given in the form of dietary supplementation (as outlined above), of anabolic steroids (body-building drugs that help to stimulate the bone marrow), and in extreme cases possibly through blood transfusions. However, this kind of intensive care is rare.

LEUKEMIA is a cancer of the blood cells and is quite common in cats. It is almost always associated with feline leukemia virus infection and is therefore described under Viral Diseases (see page 112).

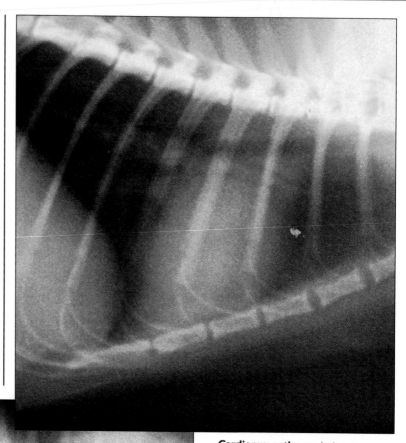

Cardiomyopathy results in a gross enlargement of the heart muscle, as seen by comparing the outline of the heart in the normal radiograph (*above*) with the abnormal heart (*left*), which is so large that it nearly fills the chest cavity. The reduced pumping capacity of the heart results in an accumulation of fluid on the chest, making the normally dark appearance of the air in the chest look whiter.

DISORDERS OF THE NERVOUS AND SENSORY SYSTEM

These are intrinsic to the cat's rapid responses.

NERVOUS SYSTEM

There is a wide range of congenital diseases of the nervous system that may affect kittens, such as *hydrocephalus*, a build-up of fluid around the brain, and *congenital vestibular disease*. The latter affects the balance of kittens and is thought to be hereditary in certain breeds of cat, including Siamese, Burmese, Birmans and British Creams. There is often very little that can be done to treat such cases, but kittens that are only mildly affected may improve with time.

FITS may be due to several causes, including:

• Injury — either directly following a knock on the head or as a delayed response days or weeks later.

• Infections that affect the brain — especially the "dry" form of *feline infectious peritonitis* (see p. 113).

• Tumors — *lymphosarcoma* due to feline leukemia virus (see p. 112) will frequently cause tumors to develop in any part of the nervous system. These may cause pain or paralysis if they are in the spine or fits if in the brain itself.

• Poisoning — fairly common in the cat due to drugs such as metaldehyde, commonly used as a slug bait.

• Epilepsy — which may have no apparent cause but might be hereditary in some cases. This is a very common problem in humans and in dogs, but it is not very common in cats.

• Other diseases — such as some forms of liver disease and terminal cases of kidney failure.

If the underlying cause of the fits can be identified and treated, it may be possible to cure them. More often than not,

however, it is necessary to resort to control with drugs rather than cure. It should be remembered that a fit is usually more distressing for the onlookers than for the person or animal having it. It is best to leave an animal having a fit in a quiet and dark place until it subsides and then seek veterinary advice. If a fit has lasted for more than ten minutes and shows no sign of subsiding, however, immediate veterinary attention should be sought. If a cat is having only infrequent fits, your veterinarian may decide against keeping the cat on permanent medication, but if fits are frequent and severe, long-term therapy may be essential. If a cat is receiving long-term medication for fits, it is important that treatment be given regularly and that it does not stop suddenly, otherwise very serious fits could follow.

Strokes in cats are not usually thought to be due to blood clots in the brain as in humans, but they may nevertheless appear very similar. Depending on the part of the brain affected, they may produce severe uncoordination, apparent blindness, or continual circling and problems with balance. These cases do not usually respond to any treatment that is given, but, as with human stroke victims, the function of damaged areas of the brain can slowly be taken over by other undamaged parts. Problems with balance may also be caused by inner ear disease, when infection has spread either from an external ear infection or a throat infection into the organs of balance in the inner ear deep within the skull. Inner ear disease will often respond well to drug treatment, although surgery to drain the deeper parts of the ear canal may be necessary in some cases.

Feline dysautonomia, also known as the Key-Gaskell syndrome, is a perplexing new disease of cats first recognized in 1981 in the United Kingdom. The cause of the disease is completely unknown, but it leads to a failure of the autonomic nervous system, the part of the nervous system that unconsiously controls body functions such as tear and saliva production, bowel movements and urination. This produces symptoms such as constipation, vomiting of undigested food, dry eyes and nose and dilated pupils. The third eyelid often protrudes across the eye, and in severe cases the cat may be unable to urinate

Feline dysautonomia causes a paralysis of the autonomic nervous system, that subconsciously controls certain body functions. This cat (*above*) shows the distinctive dilated pupils, unresponsive to light, that is typical in many cases.

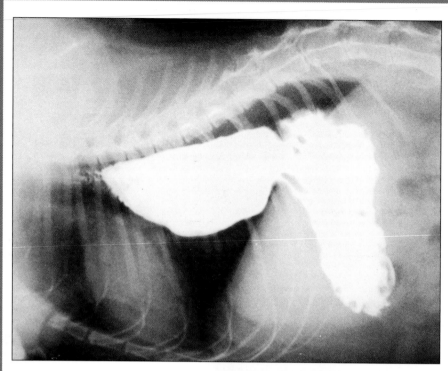

The only abnormality found in all cases of feline dysautonomia is a dilation of the esophagus, or gullet (*left*). This can be shown by giving the conscious cat a barium swallow, and then taking a radiograph immediately afterward.

White cats are particularly susceptible to skin cancer on their ear flaps due to an over-exposure to sunlight and their inherent lack of pigmenation. However, surgical treatment is usually successful and this cat (*below*) is responding well to having part of the ear flap removed, the cancer having been diagnosed at an early stage.

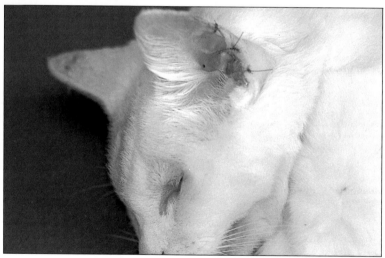

normally. Many cases show only some of these symptoms, and it is often necessary to take X-rays of the esophagus, the tube that carries food down to the stomach, since it is almost always enlarged in cases of this disease. Sometimes more than one case occurs in the same household, but very often it does not — the evidence as to whether it is infectious or not is therefore inconclusive.

Since we do not know the cause of the disease, treatment consists only of drugs to help counteract such symptoms as constipation, loss of appetite, and insufficient secretion of tears and saliva. With time, up to one third of all cases may recover and return to a relatively normal life, but some signs, such as dilation of the pupils, may never disappear. The disease is most distressing for owners, since a lot of nursing care and patience is necessary if the cat is to have any hope of recovery, and even then a fair proportion of cats will continue to waste away until they die or are put to sleep. The only encouraging aspect of this depressing disease is that the recovery rate does seem to be improving, partly perhaps because of a better understanding of how best to treat these cases, and possibly also because the disease itself is becoming milder.

EAR PROBLEMS

The ear of the cat is a very sensitive organ responsible for hearing and balance, both very highly developed senses in the cat. The ear consists of the ear flap, or *pinna*, the outer ear canal which leads down to the ear drum, the middle ear behind the ear drum which contains the three bones that transfer sound vibrations, and the inner ear, deep within the skull, which contains the organs responsible for hearing and balance.

The ear flap is very prone to tearing and injury in cat fights, or to self-inflicted damage if the cat has an ear problem and scratches vigorously with its sharp claws. This may sometimes lead to bleeding within the ear flap itself, causing the ear flap to swell up and form an *aural hematoma*. If this occurs, the cat will require an operation to drain out the blood. Otherwise the ear flap will shrivel up as the blood clot contracts within the flap, resulting in a "cauliflower ear" which may

EAR PROBLEMS

 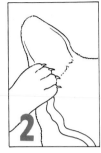 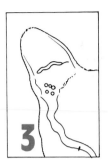 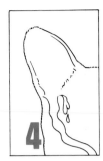 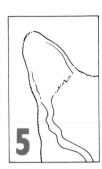

A trigger factor such as ear mites causes an irritation of the ear (**1**), which causes the cat the scratch the ear (**2**), which then causes further trauma and inflammation (**3**), allowing ideal conditions for secondary bacterial or fungal infection to grow (**4**). This may eventually lead to chronic inflammation and thickening of the lining of the ear canal (**5**).

obstruct the ear canal and cause continuing irritation. White-haired cats are prone to sunburn on the ear flaps in the warmer months of the year – this may progress to a skin cancer in that area if left untreated. Frequent applications of a barrier suntan cream and keeping the cat indoors when the sun is bright will help to prevent the problem. In severe cases it may be necessary to remove the tips of the ear flaps surgically.

Otitis externa – infection of the external ear canal – is very common in the cat. A large number of cases begin with irritation caused by ear mites (see p.115), but may then go on to become infections caused by bacteria, yeasts, or fungi. The signs to look out for are:

• Irritation – the cat will usually scratch the ear or shake its head.

• Inflammation – the skin around the top of the ear may be red and sore.

• Discharge – this may be brown, or black, or yellow, or even green!

• Smell – an infected ear often has a distinctive acrid smell.

Treatment will involve the adminstration of drops into the ear (see p. 109).

It is very important to follow carefully the directions given by the veterinarian and take the cat back for re-examination if requested. It is very tempting to stop treatment as soon as the symptoms disappear, but if the infection has not fully cleared it will soon be back with a vengeance. Pet shop remedies are best

The cat's ear consists of an ear flap or pinna (**1**) which funnels sound waves down the external auditory canal (**2**) to the ear drum (**3**). In the concealed middle ear (**4**) the ear ossicles (**5**) — the hammer, anvil and stirrup — act like a system of levers, converting weak vibrations of the ear drum into stronger vibrations of the oval window, part of the snail-like cochlea (**6**). The sound sensing organ of Corti, in which different pitched sounds cause vibrations in different parts of the organ, extends along the spirals of the cochlea. The vibrations in the organ of Corti cause nerve signals to be sent along the auditory nerve (**7**) to the brain. The semi-circular canals (**8**) comprise the balance organ (see p. 124).

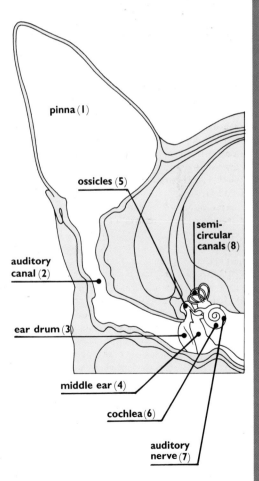

pinna (**1**)

ossicles (**5**)

semi-circular canals (**8**)

auditory canal (**2**)

ear drum (**3**)

middle ear (**4**)

cochlea (**6**)

auditory nerve (**7**)

THE BALANCE ORGAN

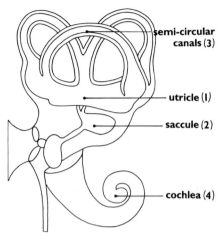

semi-circular canals (3)

utricle (1)

saccule (2)

cochlea (4)

The vestibular apparatus (*left*) is the cat's balance and orientation monitor, located in the inner ear, informing the cat which way up it is. In the chambers of the utricle (**1**) and saccule (**2**), tiny crystals of calcium carbonate press down on minute hairs, if there is any change in up or down orientation. Fluid in semi-circular canals (**3**) moves in response to any movement in direction or acceleration. All these changes are immediately signalled to the brain. The cochlea (**4**) is the hearing organ.

balance may both be affected – this is most commonly manifested by a head tilt to one side, often causing the cat to walk around in circles. Such deep ear infections are distressing for the cat and the owner and require long and extensive treatment if a return to normality is to be hoped for. Prompt treatment by a veterinarian of cases of otitis externa will usually prevent ear infections from developing to this advanced state.

EYE DISEASE

Apart from *conjunctivitis*, an inflammation of the membranes around the eye, diseases of the eye itself are relatively uncommon in the cat. Protrusion of the third eyelid across the eye is not usually a sign of eye disease itself, but signifies that the cat is generally unwell in some way (see p. 110). Sometimes it does occur on its own without any other signs of illness, and is probably due to a virus affecting the nerves that control the third eyelid. Some cats bred with a short nose, such as Persians, may have an obstruction to the flow of tears down over the face. In some cases it may be possible to clear the tear duct surgically, but it is usually sufficient to clean around the eyes regularly with cotton batting and warm water. If the area starts to become sore due to the tears, a little petroleum jelly will help to protect the skin.

avoided, because they will often soothe the ear without clearing the underlying infection. This gives a false sense of security because the cat appears better, but the infection is getting a stronger and stronger hold within the ear. Ear infections that are allowed to become well established may become very difficult to clear completely, and sometimes it is necessary to carry out plastic surgery to

open out the side of the ear canal and allow better aeration and drainage of the ear. This type of surgery may also be necessary if a cat develops growths within the ear canal.

The ear drum is a vital part of the ear and if infection causes rupture of the ear drum, *otitis media* and *otitis interna*, infection of the middle and inner ear, will follow. The cat may become unwell, and hearing and

An aural resection operation will usually provide a permanent cure to chronic and recurrent ear infections by improving the ventilation and drainage of the ear and the cosmetic appearance of the ear after the operation is generally good (*left*).

The shape of the face in many long-haired cats often impedes the drainage of tears and they tend to run down over the face (*right*). Regular cleaning of the eyes is essential to stop the skin from becoming sore.

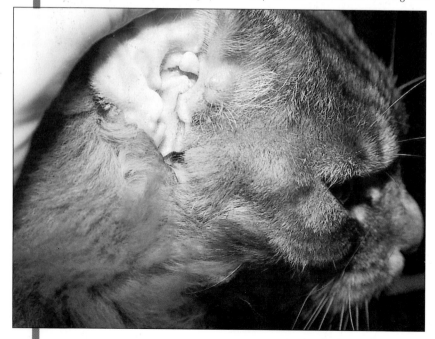

Conjunctivitis is very common in cats and may be a sign of a more generalized disease, particularly cat 'flu (see p.112). It may also be caused by a localized infection that affects only the eyes, or by some irritating agent such as excessive dust, or pollen in allergic individuals. Most cases of conjunctivitis respond well to treatment with an antibiotic ointment, sometimes combined with a drug to reduce the soreness. However, a few cases prove to be very resistant to treatment and may require long-term therapy.

Damage to the cornea, the surface of the eye, may be due to infection damaging the eye and causing *corneal ulceration*, or to injury. Any damage to the cornea will cause soreness, often cloudiness of the clear cornea, and usually cause the cat to hold its eye shut or partially shut. Any damage to the surface of the eye is potentially serious, since there is a risk that if the damage is deep it may perforate the cornea, which would probably then result in permanent blindness in that eye. The veterinarian will often put a special green dye called fluoroscein into the eye to highlight any corneal ulceration. The cornea can usually repair itself rapidly if the cause of the damage is removed and antibiotic ointment applied to control disease.

Discoloration or an accumulation of material behind the cornea or in the iris,

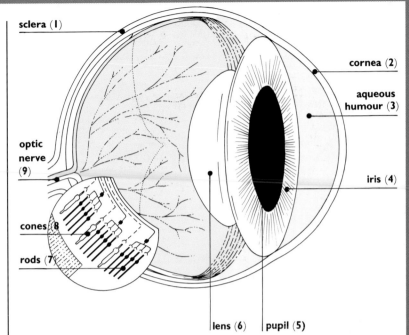

A cat's eye (*above*) is surrounded by a tough white sclera (**1**) which is replaced at the front by the transparent cornea (**2**). Behind the cornea are the aqueous humour (**3**) and iris (**4**) around the pupil (**5**). The lens (**6**) is suspended by muscles and ligaments. At the back is the retina with light sensitive rods (**7**) and cones (**8**). The optic nerve (**9**) transmits signals to the brain. The curvature of the cornea and lens plus the shortness of the eyeball give the cat a wide angle of view, compared to humans.

Conjunctivitis is an inflammation of the membranes surrounding the eyes resulting in soreness and discharge that may be due to a primary infection or irritation of the eyes (*above*). It may also be associated with a more generalized disease such as cat 'flu.

the colored part of the eye around the black pupil may sometimes be apparent. Such changes may be of little significance, but they can be a sign of a serious generalized illness such as *feline infectious peritonitis, feline leukemia virus infection* or *toxoplasmosis* (see pages 113, 112 and 137), and should always be checked by a veterinarian. If the pupil is enlarged, and does not appear to widen and narrow in response to changing levels of light, it could be a symptom of *feline dysautonomia* (see p. 120) and again should be checked. The eye is very much a "window into the body" and will often reveal signs of illness before they show elsewhere.

The lens is positioned behind the pupil and is normally transparent. However, while it is normal in elderly cats for the lens to become slowly cloudy, forming what is known as *senile cataracts.* Cataracts may sometimes cause cloudiness of the lens in younger cats following injury or other eye disease. Cataracts are also common in diabetic cats (see p. 94).

The retina is the light sensitive layer at the back of the eye. If this layer ceases to function normally, the pupil will open widely to try to let in as much light as possible — an owner may notice an increase in the light reflected from the eye. Eventually the cat may become blind. This can result from many different causes, but two causes of special interest are, deficiency of a substance called taurine, an

CATS' EYES

 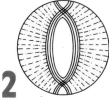 

Changes in the size and shape of the pupil may relate to the amount of light entering the eye, the mood of the cat, or possibly a disease. A widely dilated pupil (**1**), in contrast to the normal pupil (**2**), occurs in dull light or when the cat is frightened or aroused, whereas a constricted pupil (**3**) is found in bright light, and when the cat is relaxed.

amniosulfonic acid in the food — a problem with cats that are fed on vegetarian diets — and a hereditary condition called *progressive retinal atrophy* (PRA), which occurs in all cat breeds, but is commonly found in Abyssinian, Persian and Siamese breeds.

Serious damage If there has been severe damage to the eye, it may have to be removed. This tends to be of great concern to owners, who worry about how well the cat will manage after surgery and about the cosmetic effect. However, cats are able to cope with life perfectly well after the removal of one eye. Although artificial eyeballs are not a practical proposition,

the wound is usually rapidly covered with normal hair, and the cat is not likely to suffer from any psychological stress when it goes out in public! If an eye is removed, it is of course important to take extra care to insure that the other eye does not develop problems.

Blindness in both eyes will naturally pose more of a problem. If it has developed slowly, cats can learn to function in familiar surroundings quite happily. But if it has happened suddenly, as in a road accident, it is likely to cause the cat much distress. The cat is probably best put to sleep if there does not appear to be any chance of its sight returning.

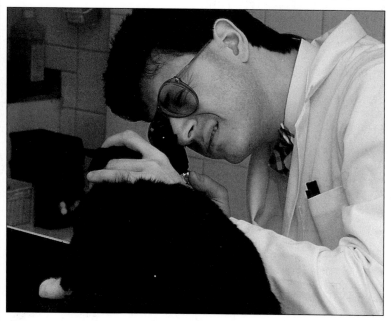

An ophthalmoscope shines a bright light into the eye, enabling a veterinarian to see a magnified image of the structures of the eye (*left*). It may be necessary to put drops in first, to dilate the pupil. Some of the changes at the back of the eye may be very subtle, and your veterinarian may wish to refer you to a veterinary eye specialist if he is unsure of the exact nature of the problem.

URINARY PROBLEMS

Malfunctions and diseases of the urinary tract are fairly common in cats. It is important to recognize when your cat is having problems urinating, as urgent attention may be essential.

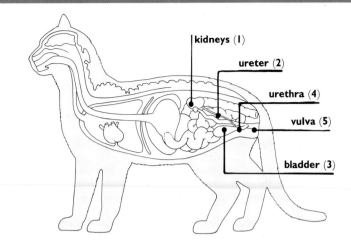

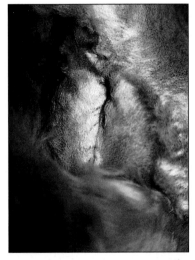

The **urinary tract** begins at the two kidneys, where urine is produced. It then passes down small tubes called the ureters to the bladder where it is stored until it is passed out via a single tube called the urethra. Disorders of the urinary tract are quite common in cats.

Kidney disease occurs mainly in the form of *chronic interstitial nephritis* in elderly cats and is therefore dealt with in Chapter 3 (see p. 97). Other forms of kidney disease may be seen in younger cats, usually producing similar symptoms. There is, however, a type of kidney disease known as *glomerulonephritis* which produces the *nephrotic syndrome*. The main symptom is the appearance of fluid under the skin of the legs and the lower parts of the body and it is sometimes referred to as "dropsy." It is important to differentiate this from the usual type of kidney failure because the symptoms are caused by an excessive loss of protein from the blood through "leaky" kidneys, and a high protein diet must be fed — exactly the opposite of the low protein diet that should be given in cases of chronic interstitial nephritis.

Cystitis, an inflammation of the bladder, is very common in the cat, and by far the most common cause of cystitis and blockage of the urethra is the *feline urolithiasis syndrome,* or FUS. The disease is due to the accumulation of a fine "sandy" material in the bladder and urethra which irritates the lining of the bladder to cause a cystitis. In male cats it will often cause an obstruction to the flow of urine down the urethra — the urethra of the female is much wider and therefore less prone to blockage. The precise cause of FUS is not clear, but it is known that it is more

The **urinary system** in both sexes, in a cat, consists of the paired kidneys (**1**) ureters (**2**) bladder (**3**) and urethra (**4**), which opens at the tip of the penis in the male whereas in the female (*above*) it opens at the vulva (**5**).

The ***Perineal urethrostomy*** operation (*left*) converts the narrow urethra of the male cat into a wide tube, resembling the female urethra so that it is less likely to become blocked with small stones. The long-term cosmetic results are usually good, and the cat usually recovers easily.

common in lazy, overweight, male cats, especially if they drink little and eat dry cat food as a major part of their diet.

Cystitis can be recognized by the fact that the cat strains frequently to pass small drops of urine, and they appear blood-stained. Very often the urinating habits of the cat will suddenly change; normally, clean cats will urinate on the rug. If the cat has a urethral obstruction, it will strain repeatedly to try to pass urine, but none will be passed. It is important to recognize this, and not to confuse it with constipation as a urethral obstruction is an emergency and must receive immediate veterinary attention.

Treatment of cystitis due to FUS involves a long course of antibiotics to clear up any urinary infection that may be present. Cystitis often recurs. The most important long-term measure to try to stop it from returning is to encourage the

cat to drink as much water as possible. A special cystitis diet may be used. Dry food should be withdrawn, and water or water and milk should be freely available in the form most attractive to the cat. Table salt added to the food will help to stimulate the cat's thirst. If the cystitis still recurs, the veterinarian may wish to X-ray the bladder to rule out other less common problems such as growths or large bladder stones, and possibly also culture the urine to discover the most effective antibiotic for the treatment of the condition. Similar preventative measures can be taken for a cat after urethral obstruction. But if the obstruction is so severe that it cannot be cleared, or if recurrences are very frequent, the veterinarian may advise an operation called a *perineal urethrostomy,* which changes the course of the male cat's urethra to bypass the narrow area near the tip of the penis.

DIGESTIVE PROBLEMS

The fastidious eating habits of the cat make it less prone to digestive upsets than the dog. Diarrhea, vomiting or constipation are common symptoms caused by a fault in the digestive system.

MOUTH

Soreness and ulceration within the mouth are quite common in cats and can be due to one or more of several causes:

• As part of a more generalized disease, particularly *feline calicivirus infection* (see p. 112) and *chronic kidney disease* (see p. 127). The former most often occurs in younger cats — in some cases the virus may cause only symptoms of ulceration in the mouth without any of the other symptoms normally associated with the cat 'flu viruses, while the latter is most often seen in elderly cats, who may also have dental problems.

• Some form of injury to the mouth from objects such as fish bones stuck between the teeth, from electrical burns due to chewing live cables, or from corrosive chemicals, which may have been directly ingested but are more often taken in while grooming the coat.

• Dental disease, usually due to the gradual accumulation on the teeth of a hard substance called tartar, formed by a combination of bacterial action on food in the mouth and chemicals in the saliva. This will build up over the years and begin to cause an inflammation of the gums, called *gingivitis*. The gums then recede, and infection is able to gain a hold around the roots of the teeth. As well as loosening the teeth, the pockets of infection may make the rest of the mouth sore. This tartar will eventually build up in all cats, but it seems to accumulate more quickly in some than in others. This is probably due partly to inherited factors affecting the nature of the cat's saliva, but it may also relate to the cat's diet. Certainly, food that exercises the teeth will at least slow down

GUMS

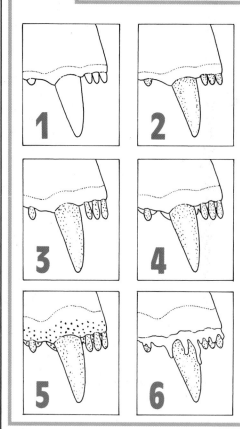

An inflammation of the gums is called *gingivitis* and often first shows where teeth and gums meet (**1**). It can be caused by a build-up of a hard coating of tartar on the teeth (**2**) which causes the gums to be pushed back (**3**), showing the base of the teeth and exposing pockets of space where food can collect (**4**), This is an ideal site for a secondary infection (**5**) and may lead to a more serious inflammation of the gums and a discharge (**6**). To remedy the situation, antibiotics, cleaning or even removal of the teeth and saline washes are needed.

this process. A small accumulation of tartar may only be a cosmetic problem, but if the gums look red and inflamed along the margins with the teeth, treatment will probably be necessary.

Treatment of a sore mouth will obviously involve an attempt to identify and remove the cause of the inflammation, with antibiotics to clear the infection that is almost always present, and possibly dental treatment under a general anesthetic to remove any teeth with infected roots and scale off any tartar that is present on the remaining teeth. Some cats seem to develop a sore mouth with no specific cause that can be identified. It is sometimes necessary to keep such cats on long-term anti-inflammatory treatment to keep the problem under control.

Not surprisingly for a species of animal that suffers from more than its fair share of tumors, growths in the mouth are not uncommon, and unfortunately they are frequently malignant and likely to spread

to other parts of the body or to regrow rapidly if removed surgically. Any unusual lumps or sores in or around a cat's mouth should be checked by a veterinarian without delay.

ESOPHAGUS

This is the tube that carries food from the mouth, through the chest and down to the stomach. Disorders of the esophagus usually cause the regurgitation of food. It is important to assist your veterinarian by watching a cat that is bringing up food to see if it is regurgitated or vomited. Regurgitation can be differentiated from true vomiting on the following grounds:

• Regurgitated food is undigested, and often is in a "sausage-shaped" mass.

• Food is usually regurgitated fairly soon after eating.

• Vomiting involves a fair amount of heaving and contraction of the abdominal muscles, whereas regurgitation is a much less violent affair.

It will often be necessary for the veterinarian to carry out a specialized X-ray, after administering a barium suspension or paste by mouth to outline the esophagus. Persistent regurgitation of food can be caused by a dilation of the esophagus, such as in *feline dysautonomia* (see p. 121), by something sharp that the cat has eaten getting stuck on the way down, by a constriction of the tube itself that may either have been present at birth or developed later on, or by an inflammation of the esophagus following an infection or the ingestion of hot or caustic substances. As with so many disorders, the first step should always be to try to determine the cause of the problem so that it can then be resolved.

STOMACH

An inflammation of the stomach is called a *gastritis*, and may often be part of a generalized inflammation of the alimentary tract, *gastro-enteritis*. It usually results in vomiting. The affected cat may also show signs of a colicky pain and refuse to eat or drink. Vomiting can be a natural function in cats to rid themselves of unwanted substances. For example, feather and bones are sometimes vomited by cats that have a soft spot for "game pie" and eat wild birds. Occasional vomiting may be nothing to worry about, but if the vomit should contain blood, and is frequent (more than once a week for

example), or if the cat is unwell, then veterinary attention is required.

Compared to the dog, cats seldom swallow objects that get stuck in the stomach because they have far more fastidious eating habits. Hair balls are a fairly common cause of gastritis, and affected cats should be groomed daily and given a dose of mineral oil or similar lubricant when necessary. Mineral oil is not absorbed from the bowel but simply "oils the works" and helps the hair to be passed on through the bowel. Some cats seem to be intolerant of certain foods and will vomit if fed them — a process of trial and error will determine what your cat can and cannot eat in such cases. Vomiting, often with diarrhea, may occur if the cat eats poison or unwholesome food. This again is to some extent a natural function to rid the body of harmful substances. Suppression of these symptoms at an early stage may mean that more of the harmful substance is absorbed into the body. However, if the vomiting or diarrhea is prolonged or very severe, they may pose a major threat to the life of the cat, and it may then be essential to use drugs to control them, and possibly intravenous fluid therapy to replace water and minerals lost from the system.

INTESTINES

Inflammation of the intestines is called *enteritis*. Enteritis primarily causes

diarrhea, possibly with blood in it. The cat may also have abdominal pain, strain to pass stools, and lose weight. It can either refuse food because it feels unwell, or eat more than normal to try to compensate for the food that is not being digested properly.

Diarrhea may be due to many causes, the most important of which are:
- Infection, when it tends to come on suddenly, may affect other cats in the same group, and often causes the cat to run a temperature and appear unwell. Feline distemper (see p. 112) used to be a frequent cause of severe vomiting and diarrhea, particularly in young cats, but now that a very effective vaccine has been available for a number of years, the disease is fairly unusual in pet cats. Other viruses, including feline leukemia virus infection, may cause less severe cases of diarrhea. Bacterial infections from other cats or from infected food may also cause diarrhea — most veterinarians will administer antibiotics, although the use of antibiotics for the treatment of diarrhea is controversial, and some veterinarians will almost never use them for such cases. Certain antibiotics can in themselves cause diarrhea, especially if administered for a long period of time. Live, unpasteurized yogurt added to the food (obtainable from a health food shop) may help re-establish "healthy" bacteria in the bowel after a course of antibiotic

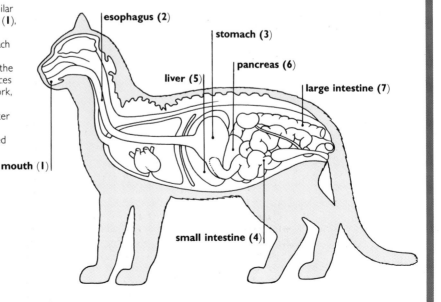

The digestive system in a cat is similar to ours. Food is taken in at the mouth (**1**), and after very little chewing is passed down the esophagus (**2**), to the stomach (**3**), where it is mixed with acid and digestive enzymes. It passes on down the small intestine (**4**), where digestive juices from the liver (**5**) and pancreas (**6**) work, together with intestinal enzymes, to break down and absorb the food. Water is then re-absorbed from the large intestine (**7**), and the feces are excreted (*right*).

esophagus (**2**)

stomach (**3**)

pancreas (**6**)

liver (**5**)

large intestine (**7**)

mouth (**1**)

small intestine (**4**)

treatment. Larger single-celled organisms called *Coccidia* are also found frequently in the intestines of cats, but they are only likely to cause problems in young kittens.

• Many cases of diarrhea are due to a problem with the diet, especially long-standing cases. Most cats will develop diarrhea if they eat too much of certain foods such as raw liver which have a laxative effect. However, other cats will develop diarrhea if they eat even small amounts of foods to which they are sensitive. While the majority of cats are fine on a diet of canned cat food, there are others who seem unable to digest it properly. This problem may apply to all canned cat foods, to certain brands, or even certain flavors of certain brands — trial and error will enable you to work out which foods agree with your cat. It is also often assumed that all cats should drink milk. However, it is not unusual for cats to be intolerant to large amounts of milk, and milk often causes diarrhea. If this is the case, the milk should either be withdrawn altogether or watered down.

Intestinal worms (see p. 135) may sometimes cause diarrhea, but this is usually a problem only in kittens.

• Growths may affect the intestines. If they are localized swellings, they do not usually cause diarrhea but may cause straining or an obstruction in the bowel. Some cats, usually elderly, may develop *alimentary lymphosarcoma*, a form of cancer of the white blood cells that is diffused along the length of the bowel and interferes with the absorption of food, causing diarrhea and weight loss. It will not usually respond to any treatment. Diagnosis of this condition can be very difficult and may involve an operation to take a small piece of the wall of the intestine for examination in a laboratory under the microscope.

• An underlying disease elsewhere in the body, such as kidney, liver, or pancreatic disease.

The treatment of any case of diarrhea is likely to involve initially the removal of any milk or milk products from the diet, and a bland diet of something such as freshly cooked chicken, or white fish fed in small amounts but often. This regime can be tried before veterinary advice is sought in mild cases if the cat is otherwise bright and eating well, but assistance should be sought if the problem persists after 48 hours.

Blood The presence of blood in the stool may be a sign of a serious problem and should not be ignored. It is important to observe the nature of the stool and the cat's behavior when they are passed. Vital assistance may be given to your veterinarian if you are able to answer such questions as:

• How often are stools being passed?
• Is the cat straining?
• Is blood streaked on the stools or mixed in with it?
• Is the blood bright red or darkly colored?
• Is the cat eating?
• Is the cat vomiting?

Although many of these questions may seem obvious, the secretive habits of many cats may mean that an owner has to be very observant to answer them reliably.

Obstruction of the intestines is not very common, but it constitutes an emergency situation if it does occur, particularly if the obstruction is at the upper end of the intestines near the stomach, since the higher up in the bowel the obstruction occurs, the more severe the symptoms.

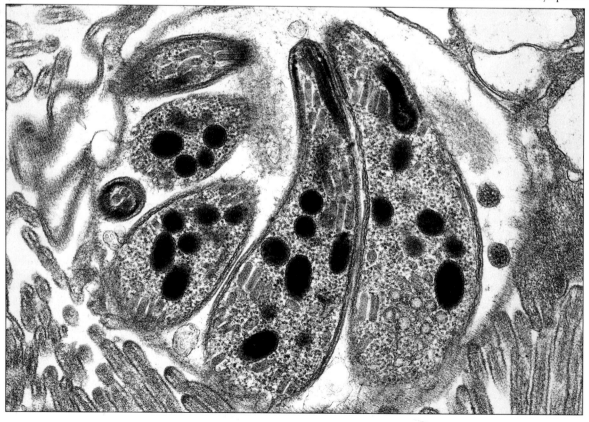

Coccidia, magnified by an electron microscope, 112,000 times, (*below, left*), are single-celled parasites that commonly cause diarrhea in cats, especially in young kittens.

Intravenous treatment with fluids from a drip (*right*) may be a life-saving measure for a cat suffering from dehydration and is unwilling or unable to retain fluids taken orally.

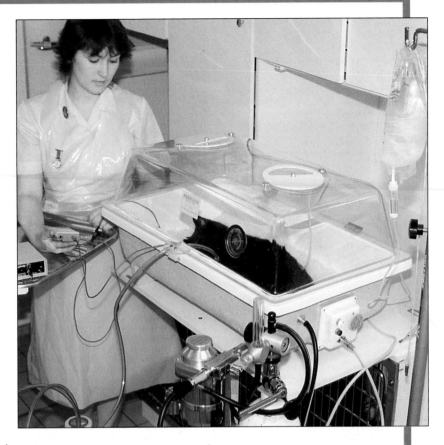

The causes of an obstruction could include a growth, a foreign object, or a twist in the bowel. When the bowel is over-excited due to diarrhea, it is possible for it to roll up on itself to cause an *intussusception*. This is not uncommon in kittens and should be borne in mind if a kitten that has had a relatively mild bout of tummy trouble suddenly deteriorates.

An obstruction should be suspected if a cat shows some or all of the following symptoms:
• Severe abdominal pain.
• Severe vomiting.
• No stools passed (stools may be passed in the early stages of the problem).
• Refusal to eat and acting unwell.
• Persistent straining without passing anything.

The diagnosis of an obstruction may be obvious on examination by a veterinarian, or it may require X-rays to be taken. Often a suspension of barium has to be administered and its progress down the intestines followed by a series of X-rays. A couple of hours may make the difference between life and death in such cases, and it is important that attention is sought without delay if the symptoms are severe.

Constipation is a very common problem, mainly in elderly cats, and is dealt with in Chapter 3 (see p. 94).

Anal sacs Occur in both sexes of cat. They are special scent glands on either side of the tail, which secrete a powerful scent onto the stools as they are passed, making them territory markers. The sacs may also be emptied if the cat is frightened. Anal sac problems are very common in dogs but quite rare in cats. Nevertheless, the anal sacs may cause irritation around the anus in cats and will then require emptying, a somewhat unpleasant task best left to the veterinarian.

LIVER

Liver problems are not very common in cats, and when they do occur, the diagnosis and treatment may be somewhat complex. However, cat owners should be able to recognize *jaundice*, a yellow pigmentation of the skin, because it may be a vital clue that all is not well and that veterinary attention should be sought. Rather like anemia (see p. 119), jaundice is not a disease in itself, but a symptom of disease that can have one of several causes. It is due to excessive levels of pigment produced from the breakdown of red blood cells, which are normally processed by the liver and then excreted into the stools, giving them their characteristic dark brown color. Jaundice can therefore be due to an excessive breakdown of red blood cells as might occur in feline infectious anemia (see p. 119), or to a failure in the processing system of the liver itself, or to a blockage of the normal route of excretion of the bile from the liver into the intestines. Yellow discoloration is often best noticed in the whites of the eyes, although it may also be visible inside the mouth, and in advanced cases, on the hairless areas of skin, such as on the underside of the abdomen. This jaundice will normally only occur if a fairly serious disease is present, and the cat should always be taken to your veterinarian for further examination to determine whether it has contracted a serious ailment such as hepatitis or pancreatitis.

PREVENTATIVE MEDICINE

There is a great deal an owner can do to lessen the chance of a pet succumbing to illness. Prevention is not only better, but in the long run often works out to be less expensive, than a cure.

? WHAT IS A VACCINE?

A vaccine contains an agent similar to the one that causes the disease. The vaccine causes the patient to develop antibodies, substances in the blood that protect the animal against that particular disease. Of course, the vaccine must stimulate this protection without causing the disease itself. The first vaccine used cowpox virus, which only causes a fairly mild disease in humans, to give protection against a very similar virus, smallpox, which is, of course, a much more serious disease. Nowadays there are two main types of vaccine:

Killed vaccines, in which the disease agent has been killed in such a way that it is still capable of stimulating protection, but obviously cannot multiply in the patient and cause illness.

Live vaccines, which contain a live virus that is either of a strain that does not cause illness, or has been modified in some way so that it is safe. Live vaccines are more likely to cause side effects than killed vaccines, but generally stimulate much stronger and longer-lasting protection.

? WHAT DISEASES CAN BE PREVENTED BY VACCINATION?

Vaccines have been developed against several viral diseases, which are particularly important to the cat:

Feline panleukopenia, also known as feline distemper, is a cause of very severe vomiting and diarrhea, especially in young cats (see p. 112). Both killed and live vaccines are available against this disease, and both are very safe and effective, but only a killed vaccine should be given to a pregnant queen. All kittens should be vaccinated against this disease, since many young cats that contract the disease will die, and regular boosting is a wise precaution.

Respiratory disease – can be caused by several different agents (see p. 118), but 80 percent of cases are caused by one of the two types of 'flu viruses, and cases caused by non-viral agents are often less severe. Therefore, in practice, the standard feline respiratory disease vaccination is generally quite effective at preventing most cats from contracting the disease, vaccinated cats that do contract the disease, generally seem to get it quite mildly. Nowadays, most veterinarians recommend routine vaccination against respiratory disease as well as feline enteritis.

There are three types of vaccine available in the United States: a live vaccine designed to be given by injection; a killed vaccine designed to be given by injection; and a live intranasal vaccine administered in the form of drops into the nose. The intranasal vaccine has some advantages over the other two types — it provides a high degrees of protection and initially only one dose has to be given to achieve very rapid protection (within 48 hours), whereas two injections of the other types, usually about three weeks apart, have to be administered to give full protection. The intranasal vaccine does quite frequently cause side effects, but this is usually nothing more than some mild sneezing a couple of days after it has been given. Because of this, many veterinarians give a combined 'flu and panleukoepenia vaccination course as a routine, but use the intranasal vaccine if a rapid protection is essential — when the cat is being boarded at short notice, for example, or if there are other cats in the same household suffering from cat 'flu. The intranasal vaccine has no other great advantage. It will also often protect at a younger age than the injectable vaccines, and may be used in young kittens that are known to be at risk.

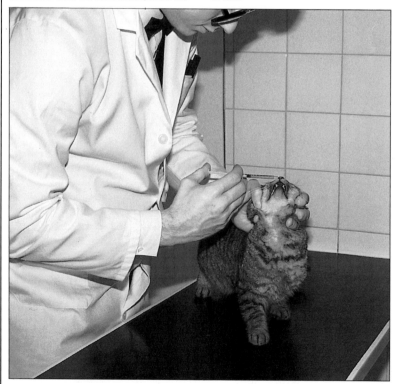

Some cat 'flu vaccines are administered as drops directly into the nose (*above*). Although there may be some side effects, this kind of vaccine provides a very rapid and effective immunity.

FELINE IMMUNOLOGY

When foreign organisms such as bacteria or viruses enter the body, they stimulate the host to produce antibodies that attach to the organisms and neutralize them (**1**). These antibodies are produced both at the site of entry — the nose or intestines — and in the bloodstream by white blood cells, the lymphocytes (**2**). Once neutralized, the organisms can be engulfed by other white cells in the blood, the macrophages, and broken down (**3**). A vaccine stimulates the body to produce antibodies so that it can respond more quickly to future infection (**4**).

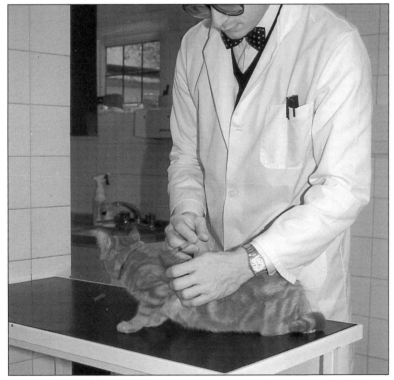

Vaccines are given by a subcutaneous injection, most commonly under the loose skin of the neck (*above*). The procedure is quick and painless, and serious untoward reactions to modern vaccines are fortunately, uncommon.

Feline leukemia virus is a very widespread virus (see p. 113) that can cause problems to develop long after initial infection and is a major killer of cats in most countries. A new vaccine is at present available in the United States and will probably become available in other countries. The new vaccine is a major step toward controlling this disease, but several injections are required, and only an estimated 80 percent of vaccinated cats are fully protected. This is certainly an area where we hope to see major advances in veterinary preventative medicine, and widespread vaccination may make this common disease a rarity in the future.

Rabies is a very serious disease that can be passed on from cats to humans. It is therefore essential that cats be vaccinated against rabies in the United States and other areas where the disease is found. Since the United Kingdom is at present free of the disease thanks to its "island status" and to stringent quarantine regulations, the Ministry of Agriculture does not permit the vaccination of animals against rabies. This is partly because of fears that routine vaccination would make the diagnosis of actual cases more difficult in the event of an outbreak. But presumably it is also to avoid fostering a false sense of security in pet owners, who might then be less vigilant against cats that do have rabies.

❓ HOW OFTEN SHOULD MY CAT BE VACCINATED?

Contact your veterinarian to discuss the vaccination regime he recommends in your area. The standard practice is usually to begin the vaccination of kittens against feline respiratory disease and panleukopenia at either nine or twelve weeks, and to give annual booster vaccinations thereafter.

❓ SHOULD I HAVE MY CAT VACCINATED FOR RESPIRATORY DISEASE EVEN IF HE HAS ALREADY HAD THE DISEASE?

Yes. The natural protection that results from a bout of respiratory disease may not last for very long, and will not confer protection against other strains of virus — *feline calicivirus* in particular has many strains. Remember, however, that the respiratory disease viruses can live in the body for a long period after an infection, and vaccination cannot be effective against any 'flu viruses that are already living in the cat's cells. Such cats are latently infected with that particular virus and may occasionally have mild bouts of respiratory disease, particularly in response to some form of stress, such as going into a boarding home. The cat may also shed the virus in its saliva and tears, so that a cat that has been vaccinated may nevertheless be carrying a 'flu virus, and may infect other unvaccinated cats.

❓ AT WHAT AGE ARE THE VACCINATIONS NO LONGER NECESSARY?

Feline panleukopenia is most common in younger cats but has been reported in older cats. Respiratory disease can occur at any age, and can be very severe in old and debilitated cats. Therefore, most veterinarians advise a combined vaccine be administered annually throughout the life of the cat.

❓ ARE THE VACCINES COMPLETELY EFFECTIVE?

No vaccine can ever be 100 percent effective, because some individuals are unable to react properly to the vaccine to produce the antibodies that are necessary to confer protection. Apart from these very rare cases, the feline panleukopenia vaccine and the rabies vaccine seem to be completely effective. As described above, the respiratory disease vaccines and the new feline leukemia vaccine are not quite as effective, but nevertheless will greatly reduce the chances of the cat becoming ill from those diseases.

❓ MY CAT WAS VACCINATED FOR FELINE DISTEMPER BUT STILL DEVELOPED GASTRO-ENTERITIS — HOW IS THIS POSSIBLE?

It should be understood that each vaccine will only protect against one agent, and similar symptoms can be due to different causes. For example, feline panleukopenia vaccine only protects against feline panleukopenia virus — it will not stop the cat from vomiting and diarrhea due to other causes.

PARASITIC DISEASES

Roundworm — are very common worms in

THE LIFE CYCLE OF A TAPEWORM

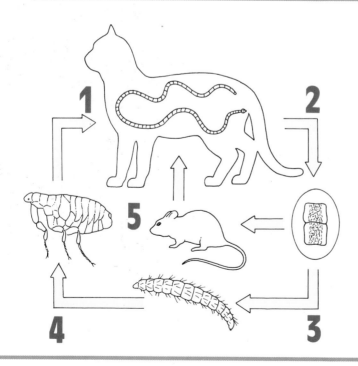

Inside a cat, tapeworms can grow up to 3½ feet long (**1**) and consist of egg-filled segments that are passed in feces (**2**). *Dipylidium caninum* eggs are eaten by lice or flea larvae (**3**) and infect the cat via the adult flea parasite (**4**). Eggs of *Taenia taeniaeformis* may be eaten by a rodent (**5**) and infect a cat that preys on the rodent, for example a rat.

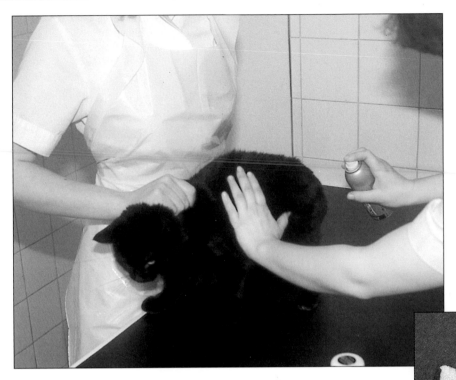

the cat and if they are passed in the stool, look like lengths of white thread. The immature worm, called larvae, lie dormant in the tissues of the pregnant queen and infect kittens by passing through the breast tissue into the milk, insuring that a large proportion of kittens become infected before they are weaned. The larvae develop into worms in the bowel, and the worms shed eggs into the stool. These eggs are very small and invisible to the naked eye – so a cat may have worms without the owner being aware of them. The eggs lie on the ground and develop into larvae, which are then either eaten by another cat, or eaten by a wild animal such as a mouse, which is in turn eaten by a cat – and so life goes on ! While many owners are not happy at the thought of their cat harboring worms, the worms rarely harm cats, except possibly when they are small kittens. All kittens should therefore be treated with a drug such as *piperazine*. It does no harm to treat adult cats occasionally, too. Piperazine is a cheap and safe drug that can be purchased from a pet shop or from a veterinarian.

Tapeworm – are also very common in the cat. The adult worm looks long and flat, like a piece of tape, although on close examination it can be seen that it is divided into segments. The adult tapeworm has hooks and suckers on its head to attach it to the wall of the bowel where it feeds on the food that the cat is so obligingly digesting on its behalf. Mature segments break off from the end of the adult worm and are shed in the stool. They resemble grains of rice but can sometimes be seen to move. These segments burst, releasing tapeworm eggs which cannot be taken in directly by another cat, but have to pass through an intermediate host first. The hosts are usually fleas but can also be lice or wild rodents.

Despite sounding and appearing somewhat horrific, tapeworm do not often harm cats much – they may occasionally cause tummy pain, appearing mildly unwell, and possibly irritation around the anus. Owners are more often aware that their cat has tapeworm, because the segments may be seen in the stools or around the cat's bottom. The worm can be more resistant to treatment than roundworm, and it is best to obtain a suitable treatment from your veterinarian, together with an insecticidal spray to clear any fleas or lice if appropriate.

Tapeworm and roundworm account for the great majority of worm infestations in cats.

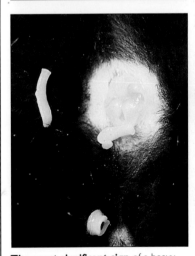

The most significant sign of a heavy infestation of tapeworm in a cat is the appearance of whitish tapeworm segments in the feces and in the area around the anus (*above*). When dry, these resemble grains of rice.

DISEASES OF CATS TRANSMISSIBLE TO MAN

Some helpful hints on how best to deal with diseases, rashes and parasites that, if you are unlucky, your cat may pass on to you.

Rabies is the most serious disease that can be passed between any warm-blooded animals. Beware of approaching stray animals and seek immediate medical attention if bitten or scratched.

Skin problems are probably the most common diseases that humans do catch from their cats, but although they can be a nuisance, they are not usually serious.

Fleas are certainly very common on cats, and will bite humans, usually causing small red spots. Flea bites can sometimes cause large red and swollen blotches on people who are very sensitive to them. Fleas seem to be very fond of biting some humans but leave other members of the same family completely alone. When they do bite, it is usually around the ankles, or sometimes on the arms, stomach and neck. Probably the worst thing you can do if you are getting bitten is to panic and get rid of the cat — even the most fastidious cat fleas will feed off a human if there is no other source of food!

Other feline skin parasites, such as lice or the Cheyletiella mite (see p. 115) are less likely to cause a skin rash on humans. Ringworm is a skin fungus that can affect humans, usually producing a red and raised ring-shaped lesion, most commonly on the arms as a result of skin contact with an affected cat. If your doctor suspects that you have caught ringworm and suggests that it may have come from your cat, ask if it is possible to have the ringworm grown in the laboratory to see what type of ringworm it is — this will give an important clue as to its source. Most cats with

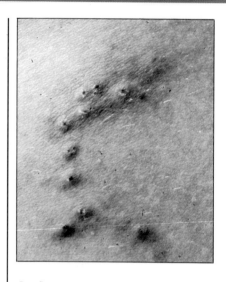

Cat fleas can leap from animal to animal and so are sometimes able to bite people, causing itchiness and red blotches on the skin (*above*).

Signs of ringworm on a cat are usually subtle and may only be visible as a small patch of broken hairs (*left*). Certain cats may even be carriers of ringworm without having the infection themselves.

Ringworm is caused by a fungus and is easily transmitted to humans, either by handling a cat or through the environment. The symptoms are circular red patches appearing on the arms (*below*) and legs that rapidly grow in size. Washing with soap and cold water is recommended initially and medical treatment is usually in the form of a fungicidal cream.

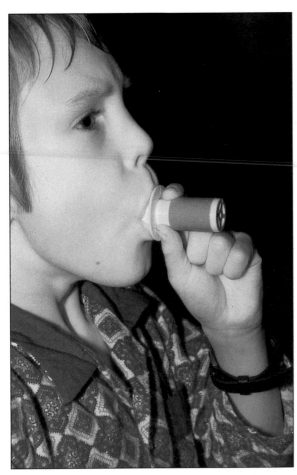

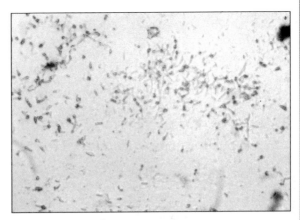

Cats' fur may produce an allergic reaction in some people, which manifests itself in an asthmatic attack (*left*). In these cases, the Rex breed of cat may make an acceptable pet because it does not shed any hair.

Cats' mouths contain certain bacteria, shown magnified 600 times (*below*), which are only dangerous if a cat seriously bites a person.

ringworm will show some signs of the disease (see p. 136), but it is possible for cats to be carriers of ringworm with very little abnormality of the coat. It is therefore very difficult for a veterinarian to examine a cat and say it is definitely free of ringworm. It may be necessary to examine the cat under a special ultra-violet light, or to send off coat brushings to a laboratory to see if ringworm can be grown.

Cowpox is a virus that normally causes sores on the teats of cattle, but it has recently been shown that it can infect cats on farms, and then be passed on to humans. Fortunately, the disease is not at all common, and is usually very mild in humans.

Cat roundworms and tapeworms are not thought to pose a health risk to humans, but there is a single-celled parasite called *toxoplasma* that often lives in a cat's bowel and sheds its eggs in the cat's stool, but it does not usually make the cat at all unwell.

Toxoplasmosis, as a disease, is due to this organism and is a possible cause of abortion in women, although it is thought that the vast majority of cases of toxoplasmosis in humans comes from handling or eating infected meat rather than from other animals such as cats. Nevertheless, it is sensible for pregnant women to take such precautions as wearing rubber gloves if they have to empty cat litter boxes. And since the eggs do not become infectious until a couple of days after they have been passed, the litter box should be emptied and disinfected daily. The danger to pregnant women from cat litter is very small, but it can do no harm to take every possible precaution.

Cat allergies can occur in humans, usually causing asthmatic symptoms. Regular grooming by someone who is not sensitive, air humidifiers and medication may help, and it is possible to have a course of injections to desensitize the patient against the allergic reaction. However, if the symptoms are severe, re-homing the cat may be the only possible course of action. Rex cats do not shed their hair, and may be acceptable to someone who is allergic to other types of cat. Many young people with allergies will grow out of them as they get older, but the advice of your doctor should be sought about such matters.

Cat bites and scratches are very common. It is always wise to insure that you are vaccinated regularly against tetanus, and it is a good idea to have your vaccinations brought up to date if you are bitten. Minor skin scratches and superficial bites will usually heal uneventfully if cleaned thoroughly with a disinfectant. However, cats can carry quite dangerous bacteria in their mouths, and if the wound is deep, or if it shows any sign of becoming infected, such as soreness, redness, pain or a discharge, seek immediate medical attention — prompt antibiotic treatment may be necessary.

BEHAVIORAL PROBLEMS

Cats can cause great inconvenience by urinating and scratching indoors — but a few tried and trusty methods, in accord with animal psychiatry — are usually successful in overcoming the problem.

? HOW CAN I STOP MY CAT FROM MAKING MESSES AROUND THE HOUSE?

First of all, it is important to distinguish between a cat that is simply urinating and defecating in the wrong place, and a cat that is deliberately spraying urine as a form of territory marking. In both cases, the cat should be watched carefully to see if it is urinating normally and passing normal stools to make sure that the problem is not due to a urinary infection or diarrhea, either of which would need appropriate treatment.

Housetraining — urinating and passing stools around the house is basically a problem with housetraining, although it may be more of a problem when the weather is very cold and the cat is less willing to venture outdoors. It may arise if a litter box is suddenly removed, or if the cat takes a dislike to the litter box. The litter box should be cleaned out thoroughly very regularly, and different types of litter tried — some cats like the smell of fresh soil in the box. The box should never be positioned close to where the cat is fed, but it may be useful to feed the cat in the areas where it is tending to soil, if necessary splitting the food into several dishes. It is useless to scold the cat after the event, but a squirt of water from a water pistol may act as a deterrent if you are able to catch the furtive culprit "in the act."

Territory — a cat will spray urine to mark its territory, and this can be recognized easily because the cat sprays standing up rather than crouching, as with normal urination, and therefore small amounts of urine will be found a few inches from the ground, against a wall, or perhaps your best sofa! Any cat, male or female, entire or neutered, may spray, but the problem is much more common in entire male cats, and the smell of tom cat urine is certainly more pungent. Spraying is also more common in households with more than one cat — the more cats, the more likely it is to occur. It can be sparked off by some form of stress, such as moving, the introduction of a new cat into the house, or having a cat flap which is allowing other cats to enter the house.

Obviously, entire male cats should be neutered, and possibly entire females as well if they are not to be bred from, since female cats are more likely to spray when calling. Your veterinarian will be able to offer you advice on the problem and may recommend treatment with hormones to help — these hormones seem to have an effect in neutered as well as entire cats. Aversion therapy with a water pistol may also be worthwhile, as well as placing food in the areas where spraying is taking place. The smell of urine is a strong stimulus to continue spraying at that same spot, and it is important to clean such areas very thoroughly. A strong solution of a biological detergent in hot water should be used, followed by alcohol, or even neat vodka. Of course, this should be tested on a small area first to be sure that it does not damage the fabric or wallcovering. The area can also be covered with aluminum foil to try to repel the cat. In some cases, the only solution is to ban the cat or cats completely from the areas in which they are spraying until they stop. If you own a lot of cats, you may have to learn to live with the problem, or reduce the number of cats in your household.

? HOW CAN I STOP MY CAT FROM SCRATCHING THE FURNITURE?

It is important to get the cat accustomed to using alternative scratching posts when it is a kitten, especially if it is to be an indoor cat. Different cats like to scratch different surfaces, but most will use a fairly large piece of carpeting firmly attached to a piece of wood. Some cats prefer it vertical, others horizontal, but it must be large enough to allow the cat to stretch out when it scratches, and it must be anchored firmly to something so that the cat can pull on it hard without moving it. That trusty weapon, the water pistol, may again be useful to deter cats that insist on using the rug or sofa. Alternatively, if you can shut the cat out of the room in which it is doing most of its scratching for a while, you may be able to break the cat's habit — declawing is a last resort.

CATS' CLAWS

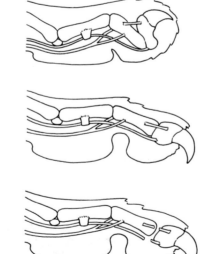

Declawing is the ultimate cure for cats that scratch the furniture, but is a fairly painful surgical procedure. In some countries, such as the United Kingdom, the procedure is considered unethical, and will only be carried out in some instances as a last resort, if the only alternative is euthanasia. The operation is more generally accepted as routine in the United States.

Scratching is normal behavior that is necessary to keep the claws sharp and to prevent them over-growing (*above*). Suitable "scratching posts" should be made available for cats that are not allowed outdoors.

Chewing houseplants should be discouraged, since many common species may be harmful (*below*). Pots of grass may provide an alternative, but as a last resort you may have to cover plants or put them out of reach.

A collar with a bell (*above*) may initially prevent your cat from catching birds, and most cats only find them a minor inconvenience.

? HOW CAN I DISCOURAGE MY CAT FROM FIGHTING?

It is natural for cats to fight to defend their territory. Fighting is more of a problem with entire tom cats than other cats because these toms will try to defend a very large territory. But it can occur with neutered cats as well, particularly when a new cat moves into the area. This is normal feline behavior and cannot be stopped, but the cats will usually settle down once they have decided on the territorial boundaries. Of course, if your cat is a tom, you should have it neutered. You may have a problem with a neighbor who refuses to neuter his own cat.

? HOW CAN I STOP MY CAT FROM BEING SO NERVOUS?

Cats' natures differ just as humans' do, and some cats will be naturally more retiring than others. It is very important that kittens become used to regular human contact when they are young, particularly from about six weeks of age. Kittens that do not become accustomed to humans at that age often grow up to be timid, especially of strangers. Plenty of kindness and patience will usually encourage the cat to become more confident, but timid cats are unlikely ever to be at ease with strangers.

? HOW CAN I STOP MY CAT FROM CATCHING WILD BIRDS AND RODENTS?

With difficulty. Just like fighting, hunting is normal feline behavior, and even the best fed cat will usually hunt just for the fun of it. A collar and bell may lower the cat's success rate, but most cats can learn to catch wild animals even with a bell on. If the cat wears a collar, the collar should have elastic in it so the cat can slip out of it if it should become caught.

? WILL IT HARM MY CAT TO CHEW AT HOUSEPLANTS?

This habit is not very good for the plants, and sometimes even worse for the cat because common houseplants, such as *philodendron* and *dieffenbachia* are poisonous. A pot of grass or catnip for the cat to chew on may help — this is particularly important if the cat is kept indoors. Smaller plants are probably best put out of a cat's reach. It may be possible to cover larger plants with cellophane until the cat has broken the habit.

FIRST AID

5

Most accidents take place in the home, for cats as well as people. Injuries can therefore be kept to a minimum by following a few simple rules to make your home safe for your cat. But even the most careful owner cannot prevent an adventurous pet from falling from heights or being hit by a car. When your cat is injured, some basic and vital knowledge of first aid, such as how to stop severe bleeding and treat shock, may mean the difference between life and death. When in pain or frightened, cats tend to be uncooperative patients and often hide. In this situation, handle your pet gently, talk to it soothingly and provide warmth and comfort until veterinary advice and treatment can be obtained.

An injured cat (*right*) being carefully lifted by the scruff of the neck and, while its body is still being supported, is gently placed into a cardboard carrying box.

EMERGENCY CARE

Some tips to help you cope with some of thé more common emergencies, which occur with cats — a great deal can be done by plain common sense before a vet has the chance to treat your cat.

❓ HOW CAN I TELL IF MY CAT NEEDS IMMEDIATE VETERINARY ATTENTION?

There is obviously a difference between a problem which makes it advisable to visit your veterinarian at the first convenient opportunity and a genuine life-threatening emergency that requires immediate attention, night or day. Some of the most common emergencies include:
• Any severe injury from a knock such as a road accident or a fall from more than about 20 feet.
• A wound that is bleeding profusely or gaping open.
• Repeated and severe vomiting, with or without diarrhea, especially if you suspect that the cat may have swallowed a foreign object (see p. 147).
• Choking.
• Severe burns and scalds.
• A fit that lasts for more than ten minutes without abating.
• Poisoning.

The treatment of these emergencies is dealt with in more detail in the following section.

In all emergencies a cool head and a large dose of common sense are vital if you are to do the best for your cat. All veterinarians are under an ethical obligation to provide 24-hour emergency service to their clients, and, if possible, you should discuss the arrangements for out-of-hours emergencies with your veterinarian before problems occur. Unless your veterinarian has told you otherwise, it is usually not a good idea to rush down to the animal hospital with the cat — telephone first to warn your veterinarian that you are on the way — you may well find that you receive a recorded message on the telephone, outlining emergency arrangements. The more urgent the problem, the more important it is to telephone first and make sure that you do not set out on a wasted journey.
• Do not abuse the emergency service that your veterinarian provides — remember that he will probably have to do a normal day's work after having been up most of the night with a difficult case. However, if you are seriously concerned about your cat and feel that its life is in danger, it is better to telephone too soon rather than too late.

❓ WHAT SHOULD I HAVE ON HAND IN CASE OF EMERGENCY?

A first aid kit for cats should contain:
Bandages — these are difficult to apply to a cat, but it may be useful to have a roll of 1 inch and 2 inch wide gauze and adhesive bandage to make a pressure bandage over a bleeding wound until assistance can be reached. Large and small gauze pads are also handy.
Sterilized cotton — useful for pressure bandages, and also for bathing abscesses. You also need cotton applicators and, to stop minor bleeding, styptic powder.
Syringe or plastic eyedropper — for administering liquid medicines. Your veterinarian will probably be able to supply you with a syringe.
Antiseptic skin ointment for dogs and cats — use one that is safe for cats, such as chlorhexidine, as the cat will often lick it off.
Mineral oil — as a treatment for hairballs or constipation; can also be used for cleaning the ears.
Washing soda or **Ipecac** — just a small amount may be needed urgently to induce vomiting if the cat swallows poison. Activated charcoal also helps.
Waterless hand cleanser — useful for removing tar or paint from the cat's coat.
Kaopectate — safe to use for mild cases of diarrhea — give a teaspoonful twice daily to an adult cat, but seek veterinary advice if the problem does not clear within 48 hours.
Cat box or basket — be sure you have one on hand so you do not have to search for it if you have an emergency.

Make sure that the telepone number of your veterinarian is readily available when needed, especially if someone else is taking care of your cat.

❓ WHAT SHOULD I DO IF I FIND A SEVERELY INJURED CAT?

• Remove the cat from the danger of further injury — do not try to administer heroic first aid in the middle of the main street!
• If the cat is unconscious, make sure that the airway is clear by cleaning any vomit, blood or other fluid from the mouth and pulling the tongue well forward. Keep the head lower than the body so that fluids can run out of the mouth and blood can circulate more easily to the brain.
• Try to control any severe bleeding by placing a pressure bandage firmly over the wound.
• Keep the cat warm by gently wrapping it in a blanket.
• Contact a veterinarian without delay.

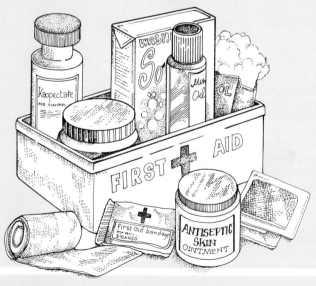

STOPPING BLEEDING

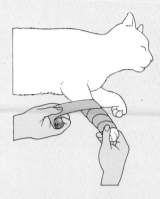

Cover a bleeding wound with some gauze, or other clean absorbent material such as a cotton handkerchief, and apply pressure for two or three minutes to stop the bleeding. A bandage may be placed firmly over the dressing until veterinary attention is available — but do not delay in seeking assistance.

An unconscious cat should have the tongue pulled forward (*above, left*) and the neck extended to allow clear air passage. Be careful to insure you are not bitten.

An injured cat should not be allowed to become cold, as it will make shock more likely. The body can be loosely wrapped in a blanket, or some modern "plastic bubble" wrapping material (*above, right*) which makes an excellent insulator.

MOVING AN INJURED CAT

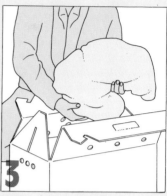

Always approach an injured cat from behind so that it does not claw you. To alleviate the possibility of putting unnecessary pressure on any internal injuries, use both hands outspread, gently coax them under the cat's rump and chest to distribute its

weight, and, avoiding any twisting or bending of the cat's body, lay the cat down onto a towel or blanket (**1**). Alternatively, (**2**), if the cat is restless, gently pick it up by the scruff of the neck, and supporting the rump, place it into a cardboard box or suitable

carrier . If the cat struggles violently, it is a good idea to wrap it up in a towel (**3**), prior to placing it in the cat carrier.

? HOW SHOULD I MOVE AN INJURED CAT?

• If the cat is lying calmly, slide one hand under the chest and one under the rump and slide the cat onto a blanket without twisting the body.

• If the cat is restless, grasp the scruff of the neck with one hand and support the rear of the cat with the other. Gently place the cat in a cat carrier or cardboard box.

• If the cat is panicky and struggling wildly, cover it with a towel or blanket, pick up the cat in it, and place the whole bundle in a sturdy box or cat carrier.

If the owner of the cat is not known, you may be able to gain assistance toward the cost of treatment from the police or the American Humane Education Society or the Society for the Prevention of Cruelty to Animals. Most veterinarians will provide emergency care for injured cats even if the owner is not known, but you should be prepared to make very effort to assist with finding the owner of the cat, and possibly to assist with the nursing of the cat until an owner is found.

? HOW CAN I TELL IF A CAT IS STILL ALIVE?

It can be difficult to distinguish between a cat that is lying unconscious and

one that has just died — the following guidelines may help you decide if the cat has died:

• The pupils of the eye become widely dilated and fixed when a cat dies and the cat does not blink if the surface of the eye is lightly touched.

• Breathing will have ceased — watch the chest to see if it moves or try holding a wisp of cotton in front of the nostrils to see if there is a flow of air.

• The heartbeat will have stopped — this can be felt on the chest in the region that lies below the elbow when it is drawn back over the chest. It may also be possible to see the movement of the body hairs in this area if the heart is beating.

If you are still unsure, it is always best to have the cat examined by a veterinarian to confirm that the cat has died.

? CAN I ADMINISTER ARTIFICIAL RESPIRATION?

If the cat is so severely injured that it has stopped breathing, it is unlikely that an untrained and unequipped owner would be able to succeed in resuscitation, and he could easily cause further internal injury if death has not already occurred. The best hope for the cat is to arrange for veterinary attention without delay.

HEARTBEAT

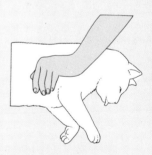

The heartbeat can be felt by holding the lower chest just behind the shoulders between the fingers and thumb of one hand, or you may be able to see the hairs moving in this area as the heart actually beats. It can be very difficult for an inexperienced person to detect if the animal is shocked and the heartbeat weak.

WHAT ARE THE SIGNS OF SHOCK IN A CAT?

Any animal that suffers a serious injury will subsequently suffer from shock to some degree, particularly if there is severe bleeding either externally from a wound or internally. A shocked cat will appear weak and sometimes shaky, with rapid, shallow breathing and pale, mucous membranes (the linings of the mouth and eyes). This condition can be fatal in itself, and urgent veterinary treatment with drugs and possibly an intravenous drip may be necessary. Do not give fluids by mouth, but help the cat to conserve its body heat by wrapping it in a blanket until assistance is available. If you have some of the plastic bubble type of wrapping material, it is ideal for conserving heat.

WHAT ARE THE MOST LIKELY EMERGENCIES I AM LIKELY TO HAVE TO DEAL WITH?

Some of the most common emergencies and their treatment are outlined below. Injuries are often caused by falls or road accidents and can include internal organ damage or fractured bones. The first line of treatment is usually to control bleeding and treat shock — only then is the cat likely to be strong enough to be examined and treated for further complications. If a cat takes a minor knock or a fall but seems fine afterward, a veterinary check-up may still be a wise precaution. However, if the cat has been knocked unconscious, is unable to walk normally, is breathing abnormally, or bleeding heavily, particularly from the mouth, anus, or in the urine, seek immediate assistance.

Rupture of the bladder is one of the most common internal injuries following an accident; it allows urine to escape into the abdomen. If this is left untreated, the cat will become ill due to the poisons it is absorbing from the urine. It is therefore very important to be sure that your cat is urinating normally if it has been involved in an accident. Your veterinarian may need to carry out special X-rays of the bladder and possibly blood tests to pinpoint the problem, and prompt surgery may be necessary.

Ruptured diaphragm is another common internal injury following an accident — the diaphragm is a sheet of muscle separating the chest from the abdomen (see p. 120). If this is damaged, the cat will have difficulty in breathing, and this may become very severe if a vital organ such as the liver or the stomach enters the chest. Surgery will be necessary to correct the tear, but the anesthetic risk is quite serious.

Fractures are very common, and can involve almost any bone in the body. Different types of accidents tend to cause different fractures. For example, while cats are able to fall from heights of up to 20 feet without injury, a cat which falls from greater heights often makes a "five point landing" on all four feet and its chin! While you may not think of looking into the mouth of a cat that has had such a fall, such falls sometimes result in a fracture of the hard palate (a split in the bones forming the roof of the mouth) or of the jaw bone. Road accidents often cause injury to the rear of the cat, commonly resulting in either a fractured pelvis or a fracture of the femur (thigh bone). Most fractures though,

SHOCK TREATMENT

One of the most important life-sustaining measures, in terms of first aid, in treatment for shock. Lay the cat down in a box or on your lap and wrap it in a soft blanket or towel, for extra warmth. Keep its head slightly lower than the rest of its body to help blood to reach the brain.

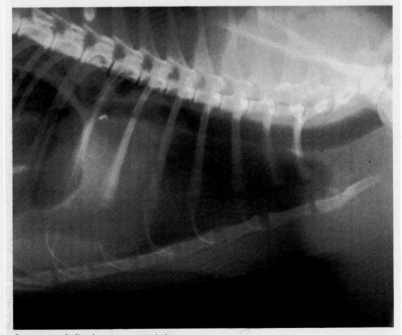

A ruptured diaphragm can only be definitely diagnosed by an X-ray (*above*). The most obvious symptom is persistent labored breathing, continuing after shock.

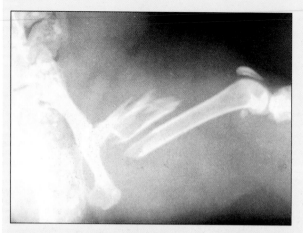

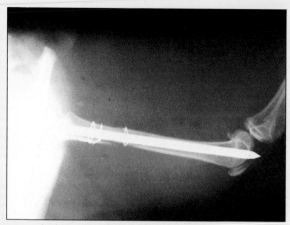

will usually heal if the cat is strictly rested for a few weeks, but careful observation is essential in the early days to make sure that there are no associated internal injuries. Fractures of the femur will usually require surgery for repair — often a metal pin is inserted into the cavity down the length of the bone to support it in position while it heals. There have been large advances in veterinary orthopedic surgery in recent years, and there is now much that can be done to repair injuries that would have been considered irreparable a few years ago.

Due to the inquisitive nature of cats and their ability to jump onto high surfaces, injuries often occur around the house. Such injuries are particularly common in kittens, and owners should be aware of the "accident black spots" in the home to try to avoid the occurence of such injuries.

Wounds are very common and should always be checked by a veterinarian. They should recieve his immediate attention if they are gaping open and exposing tissues underneath, or if they are bleeding heavily. It is difficult for an owner to assess the amount of blood that comes from a wound — a little blood can go a long way around the house.

Fight wounds inflicted by other cats are rarely emergencies unless they penetrate a vital organ such as the lungs. When an abscess from such a wound bursts and discharges pus and blood in liberal quantities, many an owner can be forgiven for telephoning their veterinarian in a panic. Such wounds should be bathed in a solution of one teaspoon salt to a pint of warm water to encourage draining, until the vet's office opens. In summer it is particularly important to insure that wounds remain clean and dry, since it is possible for flies to lay eggs on unhealthy skin, and the maggots that hatch can eat into the skin. Your veterinarian may be able to supply you with an antiseptic powder combined with an insecticide which may be useful to prevent "fly strike," particularly if the wound is around the anal region.

Gunshot wounds are unfortunately fairly common in cats, especially from BB guns and .22s, since the legislation controlling the ownership of these guns is very lax, and many youths find that cats make convenient targets. The pellet may make only a small and harmless-looking skin wound, but it may then cause serious infection or damage to internal organs.

An infected fight wound is probably one of the most common veterinary problems of all, in cats. Although they are not often dire emergencies, it is probably wise to have all deep bites treated with antibiotics to prevent sepsis developing.

The radiographs show a particularly severe fracture of the femur (thigh bone (*far left*), that has been repaired with a metal pin and wire (*left*).

Painful death may result from an air gun pellet, if it is fired at a cat. It may cause severe internal bleeding (*below*), or more commonly, serious infection. Cats, or any other living creature, should never be used for target practice.

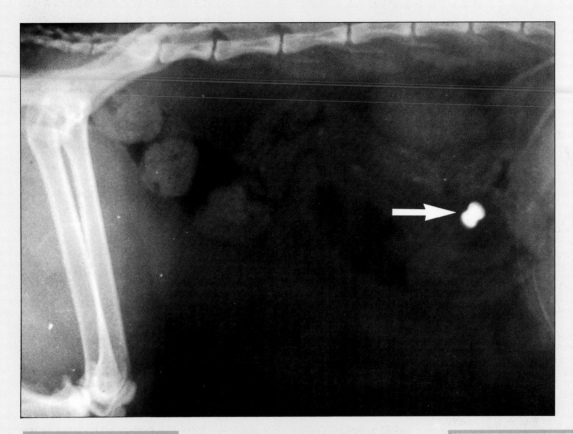

ABSCESSES

These should be bathed two or three times a day with a wad of cotton soaked in a solution of a teaspoonful of table salt to a pint of water. The solution should be used as warm as the cat will comfortably tolerate, and the wound should be gently squeezed to drain out any pus.

Choking can occur when cats chew objects, such as a needle attached to a piece of thread. They may suddenly start to gag and choke if the object lodges in the throat. Unless the offending object can be grasped easily and removed, it is usually best not to try to remove it. You may push it down the airway further by accident, cause bruising and tearing of the mouth tissues, or at the very least, receive an unintentional bite from your cat. Fortunately, while the cat may become very distressed by an object stuck in its throat, few cats suffocate before veterinary assistance can be obtained. In fact, the cat is unique among domestic pets in that they undergo a "spasm of the larynx" following a mild trauma there. This causes asthma-like symptoms that may distress both the owner and the cat.

CHOKING

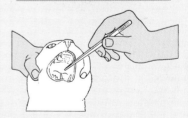

If a cat has a foreign object stuck near the front of its mouth, you may be able to remove it yourself with some tweezers. However, you may either get bitten yourself, or cause even more damage, and so it is probably best to obtain veterinary attention without delay.

BURNS

It is important that you cool down any area of burned skin immediately with copious amounts of cold water for several minutes — only then should you stop to obtain veterinary assistance.

Burns may occur when cats jump onto hot surfaces — especially ceramic cooking surfaces.

Scalds can occur when hot liquids are spilled on the cat. It is essential to cool down the skin as quickly as possible by immediately running cold water over the affected area for several minutes. Anything other than the most minor of burns should then receive veterinary attention. Electric shocks may occur if cats, or more commonly kittens, chew an electrical wire. If your cat has this habit, be sure that all electrical appliances not in use are unplugged. Sometimes an electric shock caused by chewing a wire will kill a cat outright, but usually it causes severe burns to the mouth.

● If the cat is still in contact with the wire, do not touch the cat until you have turned off the current going through the wire, or you could electrocute yourself. Veterinary attention should be sought without delay.

Heat stroke is not common in cats, since they are able to adapt to high temperatures better than dogs, but never-

theless, cats should not be left in a parked car in the direct sun or without proper ventilation. Heat stroke will cause panting, vomiting and signs of shock. The cat should be cooled down quickly with tepid water and immediate veterinary assistance obtained.

Insect stings are common, especially in the summer. They usually occur on the face or on the feet and result in a fair degree of pain and swelling. Bee stings should be bathed in a cold bicarbonate of soda (baking powder) solution and the sting removed if it is found; wasp stings should be bathed in vinegar. Most stings are not very serious and will soon get better by themselves, but some cats can be allergic to stings and swell up alarmingly. Veterinary attention should be sought in these cases, or, if the sting is in the mouth, where swelling may interfere with the cat's breathing.

Drowning is not very common. Although most cats (except supposedly the Turkish Van breed) do not like water, they can swim if they have to. If you should discover a

drowned cat, try to drain the water from its chest by holding it upside down by its hind legs and swinging it up in front of you. The centrifugal force will help the water drain out of the lungs and hopefully stimulate breathing. If there is any sign of life, veterinary assistance should be obtained immediately.

Fits are not very common in cats and usually only last a few minutes. The cat is best left quietly in a darkened room. It should be checked afterwards to try to discover the cause of the fit. However, immediate attention should be sought if the cat may have eaten poison, has had a serious injury, or if the fit continues for more than ten minutes without showing signs of abating.

Trapped cats are not as common as may be thought — a cat skeleton has never been found in a tree! While it is true that cats find it easier to grip when climbing up trees than when climbing down again, they are usually able to get down from trees if left alone, and serious injuries due to cats falling from trees are very unusual. Unless

Descent may look impossible (*left*) but a cat will usually manage if left to its own devices. A cat will often move even further along a branch to avoid an intrepid rescuer climbing up on a ladder!

DROWNING

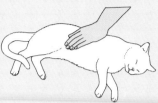

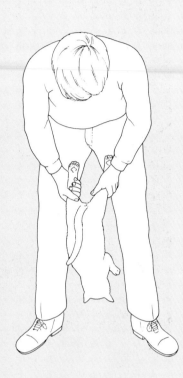

If the cat is showing no signs of life when it has been pulled out of the water, resuscitation can be attempted while veterinary attention is being sought. The cat should be held upside down by its hindlegs and gently swung to drain the lungs of any water. If the cat is still not breathing it should be laid on its side and the chest pressed rapidly several times. Keep doing this repeatedly, stopping to check the heartbeat to see if the cat is breathing yet.

PAW PROBLEMS

You may be able to remove a foreign object stuck in the paw with tweezers, but most cats will not readily cooperate. As antibiotics may be needed, you should consider help in performing the task from the veterinarian.

a cat is obviously distressed, it is usually best to wait for up to 24 hours before assuming that the cat really is stuck and calling the local fire station. Unless you can easily and safely reach the cat with a ladder, do not attempt an heroic rescue yourself, particularly at night. It is possible for cats to become trapped in drainage ducts or ventilation shafts and it may be impossible to free them because they panic and struggle violently when handled. In these cases it may be necessary for a veterinarian to administer a sedative injection before the cat can be freed.

Poisoning in cats occurs because, while cats are fastidious in their taste, they are susceptible to many poisons that do not harm other species such as the dog. Due to their grooming habits, they are also prone to swallow harmful substances that have settled onto their coats by accident. Therefore, you should seek immediate veterinary advice if you believe your cat has either eaten or walked in a substance that may be poisonous — it may be too late if you delay until the cat is actually unwell. The treatment for poisoning will depend very much on the nature of the poison itself, and it is therefore important to find out as much about it as you can.

DANGERS IN THE HOME

Cats are naturally cautious and tend to avoid poisons. But toxic substances may be taken in by a cat simply grooming itself and cat-owners should be on their guard to detect early symptoms.

Some common substances that are poisonous to cats include:

Weedkillers can be harmful to cats, especially *sodium chlorate*, which will cause diarrhea, abdominal pain, blood in the urine and sometimes even death.

Rodenticides, used to control rats and mice, are probably the most common type of poison to be eaten by cats, either directly, or perhaps by catching and eating a rodent that has eaten the bait. The most common types of poison are those that interfere with blood clotting. These compounds cause symptoms due to internal bleeding; vitamin K injections can be given to counteract their effect.

Alphachloralose is also commonly used as a mouse bait. It can cause signs of either over-excitement or drowsiness and kills mice by allowing their body temperature to drop to a fatal level. Therefore, an essential part of the treatment for this poison is to keep the cat warm while it is recovering.

Fortunately, the use of the more old-fashioned and highly toxic poisons for killing rodents such as *strychnine, thallium*, and *fluoracetate* is strictly controlled in the United States. Many of the drugs are color-coded with dyes by the manufacturers to aid in their identification; the color of any poison that is found, or even seen, in vomit, should be passed on to your veterinarian.

Slug bait pellets usually contain *metaldehyde* and are often eaten by cats, although some of the modern preparations contain substances that repel pet animals. The drug causes lack of coordination, muscle twitching, excessive salivation, possibly leading to collapse and unconsciousness.

Drugs are a problem because cats are very sensitive to many drugs that are safe for other species, and medicines should only be given on the advice of your veterinarian unless you are certain they are safe for your cat. Do not store prescription medicines after the course of treatment for which they were prescribed has been completed, and do not give medicines that have been prescribed for one animal to another.

Two of the most common painkilling drugs for humans are *aspirin* and *acetaminophen*, both of which are found as a component in a wide variety of medicines. They are both highly poisonous to cats. Aspirin causes severe vomiting and diarrhea, excitement and even convulsions, and acetaminophen causes blood disorders.

Insecticides are commonly applied to cats to control parasites, and problems may occur if drugs that are not specifically approved for cats are used, or if the correct drugs are used in the wrong dose. Always read the directions thoroughly before applying an insecticide, and do not apply more than one drug at the same time — a particularly common error when a cat is wearing a flea collar. Flea collars may sometimes cause a skin irritation in cats that are allergic to them.

Household agents may often present a hazard to cats, especially if they are spilled on the skin and then licked off. Examples of poisonous substances include bleach, gasoline, shoe polish, some crayons and pencils, and many of the detergents and cleaning agents available. It is important to wash any such substances off the cat thoroughly with large amounts of water. Oil-based substances such as gloss paint should not be removed with turpentine or turpentine substitute, which is poisonous and an irritant in itself, but with waterless cleansing agent or butter or vegetable oil, which should then be washed off.

Anti-freeze contains *ethylene glycol*, which is sweet-tasting and quite palatable to many cats, but is unfortunately also very poisonous. It may cause lack of coordination, difficulty with breathing, and coma. Lower doses may not cause such obvious signs but may cause kidney failure due to the formation of crystals in the kidneys. Prompt and intensive treatment is essential.

Phenolic compounds are especially poisonous to cats even in small amounts because cats lack the ability to get rid of them safely from their bodies. They are found in a large number of *disinfectants* and *wood preservatives* such as creosote and tar. Many commonly used disinfectants can be harmful to cats. Your veterinarian may be able to offer you advice or even supply you with a suitable disinfectant if you have a problem obtaining one that you are sure is safe to use.

Wood preservatives can be harzardous to cats. If fences and sheds are being treated, either try and keep inquisitive cats indoors or use a preservative that is known to be safe.

Poisonous gases such as carbon monoxide from car exhaust and smoke from a household fire may affect cats. Obviously, the first step is to move the cat into the fresh air, and then to obtain veterinary treatment.

Plants may be poisonous, but most cats are too fastidious to eat any that are harmful. However, cats that live indoors may get into the habit of chewing houseplants (see p. 139). A wide range of plants are potentially poisonous to cats. They include:

Alocasia	Crown-of-Thorns
Amaryllis	Cyclamen
Arrowgrass	Daffodil
Autumn Crocus	Dieffenbachia
Avocado	Foxglove
Azalea	Holly
Baneberry	Horse chestnut
Bear grass	Hyacinth
Bird of Paradise	Hydrangea
Black-eye Susan	Iris
Black Locust	Ivy
Bleeding Heart	Jessamine
Bittersweet	Jonquil
Bloodroot	Laburnum
Bluebonnet	Laurel
Boxwood	Lily of the Valley
Burning Bush	Mistletoe
Buttercup	Mountain Laurel
Caladium	Peach
Castor Bean	Philodendron
Cherry Laurel	Pine needles
Chinaberry	Poinsettia
Christmas Rose	Rhododendron
Cornflower	Wisteria
Corydalis	Yew
Crocus	

Poisoning with mushrooms such as Fly Agaric and False Blusher has also been reported.

The general principles of First Aid for any poisoning are:
• Identify and remove the source of the poison — keep a sample if possible.
• Administer an *emetic* to induce vomiting without delay — a pea-size lump of washing soda is best, but a strong salt solution may work. *Do not* administer an emetic if the cat is unconscious or if a corrosive or irritant substance has been swallowed. With irritant poisons, a demulcent mixture, such as milk and egg-white or olive oil can be given to soothe the stomach but veterinary advice should be sought first if possible.
• Arrangements should be made to take the cat to a veterinarian.

PLANTS TO AVOID

Some popular garden plants that are poisonous and your cat should avoid are: Iris (**1**), Ivy, *Hedera*(**2**), Cornflower, *Centaurea* (**3**), Bird of Paradise, *Strelitzia* (**4**), Christmas Rose, *Heleborus* (**5**), Laburnum (**6**), Foxglove, *Digitalis* (**7**), and Yew, *Taxus* (**8**).

Homes may be dangerous places for a cat, who is naturally curious and inquisitive and often, initially, through lack of experience, unaware of potential hazards. In a typical kitchen (**1**) accidents may be caused by pans of boiling water or hot fat that a cat is capable of spilling, open doors, such as the washing machine, drier and oven, which may attract cats by their warmth, open cupboards containing poisons detergents and cleansers and rubbish bins that may contain small bones that could lodge in a cat's throat. In living areas (**2**) there are potential dangers from electrical cables that some cats like to chew. Open doors leading to high balconies, objects precariously resting on tables and shelves laden with precious ornaments should definitely be avoided. In general (**3**) watch out for fires without guards, poisonous houseplants and open drawers in which a cat may be accidentally trapped.

VETERINARY RECORD SHEET

Name of Veterinary Practice: ....

Practice Address: ....

Practice Telephone Number: ....

Emergency Telephone Number: ....

Name of Cattery: ....

Cattery Address: ....

Cattery Telephone Number: ....

MEDICAL RECORD

Name of Cat: ....

Breed: ....

Date of Birth: ....

VACCINATION PROGRAM	DATE	PREGNANCY	DATE
Feline panleukopenia		Mating	
Feline leukemia		Veterinary check	
Rabies		Birth	
Deworming		Neutering	
Boosters			
		General Health Notes	
		Major illness	
		Hospitalization	

GLOSSARY

Abdominal cavity The space in the body, behind the diaphragm that contains organs such as the liver and intestines.

Abortion The expulsion of a fetus before it is fully developed.

Abscess A collection of pus below the skin, surrounded by inflammation.

Agouti The sandy color, found between the black stripes of a tabby.

Alopecia Baldness.

Anemia A reduction in the number of red blood cells that may be due to a number of causes.

Angora An out-of-date term used for Persians, now reserved for Turkish breeds.

Antibody A substance produced by white blood cells to neutralize foreign proteins such as bacteria and viruses.

Anticonvulsant A drug that is used to control fits.

Ataxia Uncoordinated movements.

Autonomic Nervous System The part of the nervous system that controls subconscious functions such as the digestion of food.

Aversion therapy Changing a particular behavior pattern by teaching the animal to associate the behavior with an unpleasant stimulus, such as spraying with water.

Back-cross Mating back of offspring to a parent.

Barbiturate A type of drug used as a sedative, an anticonvulsant, or as an anesthetic. It is also commonly used for painless euthanasia.

Bile A substance excreted by the liver to aid the absorption of fats from the bowel.

Bloodline Cats which are related to each other, through various generations.

Breed A group of cats with similar defined physical characteristics and related ancestry.

Calling The term used to describe a female cat in season, since she will often make yowling noises to attract male cats.

Cancer An abnormal, uncontrolled growth of a group of body cells.

Canine teeth The long sharp teeth near the front of the mouth used for catching and killing prey.

Carrier An animal that is able to pass on infection, but is not showing any clinical signs of that infection.

Carry Genetic expression, relating to the presence of a gene which is not evident in the appearance of a particular individual.

Cat Fancy Selective breeding and exhibiting of cats.

Cross breeding Mating of two, usually pedigreed, varieties.

Cocoon A tough covering that some insects, such as fleas, make to protect themselves during their development before they hatch out as adults.

Congenital A disorder that is present at birth.

Dam Mother cat.

Dehydration A reduction in the water content of the body due to excessive loss or inadequate intake of water.

Dermatitis An inflammation of the skin, sometimes called eczema.

Dyspnea Labored breathing.

Entire Unneutered.

Estrus Breeding period of the female.

FCI Feline calicivirus — a respiratory disease linked to FVR.

FeLV Feline leukemia virus.

Feral cats domestic cats that have become adapted to living in the wild.

FIA Feline infectious anemia.

FIP Feline infectious peritonitis.

Foreign Description applied to cats with a lithe, fine-boned body, as exemplified by the Siamese.

FPL Feline panleukopenia — also known as feline distemper.

FVR Feline respiratory disease called herpesvirus.

Genes The unit of heredity that controls all the physical characteristics with which an animal is born.

Gestation Pregnancy.

Ghost markings Faint tabby pattern seen in young kittens which soon disappears.

Haw 'Third eyelid'; nictitating membrane.

Heat Female's period of estrus.

Hepatitis An inflammation of the liver.

Hereditary disease A disease that is passed on by the genes from generation to generation.

Heterozygous Having a non-matching pair of genes controlling a particular characteristic — only the dominant gene will be expressed.

Homozygous Having an identical pair of genes controlling a particular character.

Host The animal upon which a parasite lives.

Immunity The ability of the body to protect against infectious disease.

In-breeding Crossing of closely related cats, for example, brother and sister.

Incontinence An inability to control the passing of feces or urine, or both.

Incisors The small teeth at the front of the mouth used for tearing food and grooming.

Infertile Unable to breed.

Insecticide Chemical used for killing insects such as fleas and lice.

Jaundice A yellow coloration of the body tissues, with bile pigments, due to one of several causes.

Larva An immature stage in the development of many insects such as fleas.

Leukemia Cancer of the white blood cells.

Membrane A thin sheet of tissue.

Molars The large chewing teeth at the back of the mouth.

Mongrel Cat with no fixed pedigree.

Nephritis An inflammation of the kidneys.

Neutering Surgical removal of the sexual organs — spaying, or ovariohysterectomy in the female, and castration, or orchidectomy in the male.

Nictitating membrane Membrane present at the side of each eye nearest the nose, which usually becomes apparent in cases of illness and debility when it partially extends across the eye.

Odd-eyed Having two eyes of a different color.

Oriental Used in association, or interchangeably with foreign to denote type.

Pads The leathery undersides of cats' feet.

Pancreatitis An inflammation of the peritoneum, a membrane that lines the abdominal cavity.

Phenotype The appearance of the cat, such as its color or hair length, as a reflection of its genetic make-up.

Pinking up Expression used for the development of the pregnant queen's nipples.

Pneumonia A lung infection.

Points Colored regions of the body, typically associated with Siamese cats.

Queen A female cat that has not been neutered.

Reflex action A very rapid response to a stimulus that occurs without conscious control by the brain.

Registration The recording of a kitten's birth, giving appropriate details such as its ancestry, with a governing body.

Rumpy Description used for a Manx, which has no tail.

Self Coat of one even color.

Sex linkage Genetic trait associated with the sex chromosomes.

Shock A cardiovascular disturbance that follows on from serious injury.

Spaying Surgical removal of the female reproductive organs to prevent a queen from having kittens.

Stud Male cat kept for breeding, or breeding premises themselves.

Stumpy Remnants of a tail in the Manx.

Tabby markings, either striped, spotted or blotched.

Tartar A hard mineral deposit that accumulates on the teeth.

Ticking Banding seen on the hairs of Abyssinians.

Tipped Ends of individual hairs of a different color to that at the base.

Tom Intact male cat.

Tranquilizer A drug that reduces anxiety.

Variety Specific color form or other characteristic within a breed, but the term often may be used in place of breed itself.

Vasectomy A surgical operation to cut the tubes carrying sperm from the testes to the penis, making an entire male cat infertile.

Virus The smallest of all living particles, only capable of multiplying inside other cells.

INDEX

ACKNOWLEDGMENTS

The publishers acknowledge the cooperation of photographers, photographic agencies and organizations listed below.
Abbreviations used are: t top; c center; b bottom; l left; r right; u upper; lw lower.

8 Trustees of the British Museum; **9** (cr) Mike Brucelle; **10-11** Marc Henrie; **13** Sally Anne Thompson; **14** Marc Henrie; **18** Marc Henrie; **19** (tl) Sally Anne Thompson; (c) Marc Henrie; **20-21** Marc Henrie; **22** Sally Anne Thompson; **27** Marc Henrie; **28** Sally Anne Thompson; **31** (bl) Bradley Viner; **32-33** Bradley Viner; **34** (cr) Bradley Viner; (bl) Spectrum; **36** Marc Henrie; **37** Glaxo; **38** Bradley Viner; **39** Bradley Viner; **42** Bradley Viner; **46** (t) Sally Anne Thompson; **47** (tr) Marc Henrie; **50-51** (b, c, lw r) Marc Henrie; **54** (t) Paul Forrester; (b) Mick Hill; **55** Animals Unlimited; **57** Bradley Viner; **58-59** Bradley Viner; **63** Marc Henrie; **64** Bradley Viner; **65** (l) Bradley Viner; (r) Marc Henrie; **66** (l) Sally Anne Thompson; (r) Bradley Viner; **67** (t) Sally Anne Thompson; (r) Creszentia Allen; **69** (c) Sally Anne Thompson; (lw l) Bradley Viner; **72-73** (ct) Paul Forrester; (lw r) Marc Henrie; **75** Bradley Viner; **77** Sally Anne Thompson; **78** Marc Henrie; **80** Marc Henrie; **83** (t) Sally Anne Thompson; (lw r) Bradley Viner; **85** Marc Henrie; **87** (t) Marc Henrie; (lw r) Bradley Viner; **88** Bradley Viner; **89** Bruce Coleman Ltd; **91** Marc Henrie; **93** Bradley Viner; **95** Bradley Viner; **96-97** Bradley Viner; **98-99** Bradley Viner; **103** Bradley Viner; **104-112** Bradley Viner; **113** Science Photo Library; **115-127** Bradley Viner; **130** Science Photo Library; **131-133** Bradley Viner; **135** (t) Bradley Viner; (cr) Glaxo; (lw r) Bradley Viner; **136** (t) Glaxo; (lw l, r) Bradley Viner; **137** John Watney; **139** Marc Henrie; **141-147** Bradley Viner.
All other photographs property of Quarto Publishing Ltd.

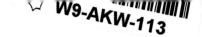

Fijian Dancers
On The
Beach

FIJI

BY KATHRYN STEVENS

THE CHILD'S WORLD®

COVER PHOTO

A Fijian schoolgirl.
©Morton Beebe/CORBIS

Published in the United States of America by The Child's World®
PO Box 326
Chanhassen, MN 55317-0326
800-599-READ
www.childsworld.com

Project Manager James R. Rothaus/James R. Rothaus & Associates
Designer Robert E. Bonaker/R. E. Bonaker & Associates
Contributors Mary Berendes, Dawn M. Dionne, Katherine Stevenson, Ph.D., Red Line Editorial

The Child's World® and Faces and Places are the sole property
and registered trademarks of The Child's World®.

Library of Congress Cataloging-in-Publication Data
Stevens, Kathryn, 1954–
Fiji / by Kathryn Stevens.
p. cm.
Includes index.
ISBN 1-56766-907-7 (lib. bdg. : alk. paper)
1. Fiji—Juvenile Literature.
[1. Fiji]
I. Title.
DU600 .S77 2003
996.11—dc21

00-013184

Table
of
Contents

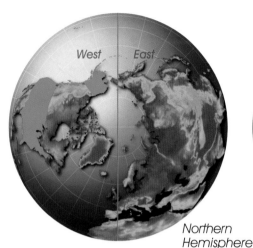

Northern Hemisphere

Fiji (white, circled) is in the south and east and U.S.A. (green) is in the north and west

Southern Hemisphere

Viewed from high above, Planet Earth has large land areas, called **continents**. The continents are surrounded by blue oceans. Smaller islands of land lie within the oceans. Many islands dot the southern Pacific Ocean. One group of these islands makes up the nation of Fiji.

Fiji's islands lie directly east of Australia. Between Fiji and Australia are the islands of New Caledonia and Vanuatu. Other islands, including Tonga and Samoa, lie to Fiji's east. Fiji has 332 islands and smaller islets, but only about 100 are **inhabited** by people.

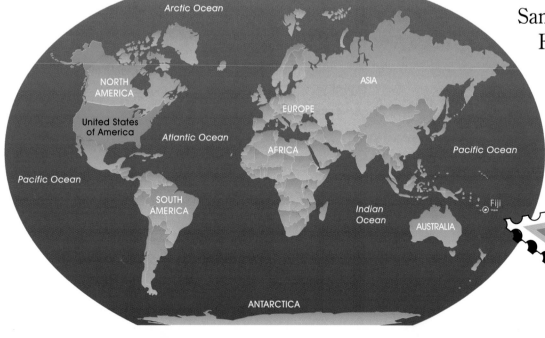

The World Shown Flat

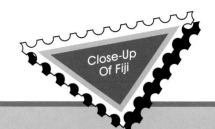
Close-Up
Of Fiji

SOLOMON ISLANDS

VANUATU

SAMOA

FIJI   TONGA

NEW CALEDONIA

AUSTRALIA

South Pacific Ocean

NEW ZEALAND

Farmland
And
Mountains
Near
Nakoro

YASAWA ISLAND

•Nakoro

©Buddy Mays/CORBIS

The Land

Fiji's beautiful islands have green mountains, waterfalls, grassy plains, white sandy beaches, and clear blue water. Over 90 percent of Fiji's people live on the two largest islands, which contain over 85 percent of Fiji's land. All of Fiji's larger islands were formed by ancient volcanoes where hot, melted rock leaked out through Earth's crust. Other smaller islands, slowly built up by sea creatures called coral, barely rise above the sea.

Fiji's **tropical** weather is warm and moist all year. The warmest summer months—December through February—are also the rainiest. The islands' **windward** south and east sides are wetter and cooler because they face into the moist ocean winds.

The **leeward** north and west sides are dryer because they are more sheltered from the winds. Between November and April, Fiji is sometimes hit by cyclones—tropical storms with heavy rains and damaging winds.

Palm Trees Border A Beach On Yasawa Island

©Craig Lovell/CORBIS

A Waterfall In The Forest

©Jack Fields/CORBIS

Almost half of Fiji's land is forested. The moist windward sides of the mountainous islands have thick green rain forests. The drier leeward sides have grasslands. Colorful flowers, including orchids, hibiscus, and cannas, grow everywhere. Common trees include coconut palms, mangroves, hardwoods, and fruit trees such as guava and orange.

A Green Sea Turtle

At one time, the only mammals that lived on Fiji were bats and rats. Early settlers brought dogs, goats, cattle, and many other animals. Fiji has lots of birds from colorful little parrots to over a hundred other types. Snakes are common, and so are lizards. Underwater, Fiji's spectacular coral reefs are home to beautiful angelfish and many other sea creatures.

©Dave G. Houser/CORBIS

Suva

A Regal Angelfish

A Native
Fijian Greeting
The Duchess
Of York
In 1927

Suva

©Bettmann /CORBIS

Long Ago

Fiji's first settlers arrived from other South Pacific islands about 3,500 years ago. These hardy islanders took huge canoes out onto the ocean to fish. They lived in tribes, each headed by a leader called a chief. Warfare between the tribes became common.

European explorers spotted Fiji's islands in the 1600s. But the explorers spent little time there until the early 1800s, when valuable sandalwood was discovered. This sweet-smelling wood was used for making soaps and perfumes.

Then came European missionaries working to spread the Christian religion, and European planters who wanted to grow sugarcane and cotton. Fiji's leader finally turned over control of the islands to Great Britain in 1874.

A Fijian Club Dance In 1840

The new British governor allowed the Fijian chiefs to keep governing their own villages and lands. He also said that lands belonging to Fijians could not be sold and that the Fijians could not be used as laborers. Instead, **indentured servants** were brought from India to work on the farms.

Fiji became an independent nation in 1970, and its history since then has been troubled. The biggest problem has been tension between the islands' Indian and native Fijian peoples. Great Britain left the native Fijians in control of most of the land. Indian residents could rent the land but never own it. By 1987, Indians slightly outnumbered native Fijians and gained control of the government. Just a month later, the Fijian-controlled army took over the **parliament** and staged a **coup**.

A new **constitution** in 1990 gave Fijians control of the presidency and the parliament. This lasted until 1998, when a new constitution guaranteed seats in parliament to native Fijians, Indians, and others.

The country's first Indian prime minister was elected in 1999. But problems continued. In 2000, a rebel leader took over parliament and held the prime minister and other leaders **hostage** for almost two months.

Dr. Timoci Bavadra, Former President Of Fiji

2UE

Levuka

Storefronts
Of Levuka

A Man
De-Husking
A Coconut
At The Fiji
Cultural Center
On Viti Levu

Wakaya Island

VITI LEVU ISLAND

Almost half of Fiji's people are native Fijians. Nearly as many are Indo-Fijians descended from the Indians who came to work on farms. A small number are from China, other South Pacific islands, Europe, or other places. Native Fijians and Indo-Fijians do not enjoy a good relationship and rarely intermarry.

People's religions in Fiji tend to reflect their backgrounds. Indo-Fijians have tended to keep the beliefs thier families brought from India. Most of them follow the Hindu religion, and a smaller number are Muslims. Most native Fijians adopted Christianity as their religion under the influence of missionaries. Before they adopted Christianity, they followed traditional beliefs in spirits or gods.

©Ted Streshinsky/CORBIS

A Young Indian Woman

©Robert Holmes/CORBIS

Two Meke Dancers On Wakaya Island

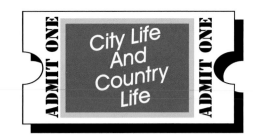
About two-fifths of Fiji's people live in cities and towns. In recent years, many people have moved from villages to towns, but they cannot always find jobs there. Most of Fiji's towns are near agricultural land and good harbors.

Suva, the largest town, has 141,000 people. Its buildings include both modern high-rises and old buildings left from the days of British control. Today, city dwellers' houses range from modern homes to poorly built shelters.

The other three-fifths of Fiji's people live in the countryside, mostly in small fishing or farming villages. Years ago, Fijian village homes were one-room houses called *bures*. The *bures* had **thatched** roofs of leaves or reeds, and walls of woven mats. The largest house belonged to the village's chief. More modern village houses have tin roofs and walls of plywood or concrete blocks. These homes withstand cyclones better than the older structures.

©Dave G. Houser/CORBIS

A Traditional Bure House In Vuaki

Vuaki

Suva

©Wolfgang Kaehler/CORBIS

Fijian
Children Doing
Schoolwork In
Nakavu
Village

Nakavu   Levuka
VITI LEVU ISLAND

A Student Solving A Math Problem In Levuka

©Robert Holmes/CORBIS

Over 90 percent of Fiji's people can read and write. Fijians are not required to go to school, but almost all children attend primary school. Education is free for the first 8 years. Students must pay for grades 9 to 12, but most are still able to attend. After secondary school, some students go on to a trade school, and some go on to a university or medical school.

Fiji's official language is English, and almost everyone can speak it. But Indo-Fijians often speak to each other in a **dialect** of Hindi (HIN-dee), an Indian language. Fijians often speak to each other in Fijian.

A Schoolhouse On Viti Levu

©Craig Lovell/CORBIS

Fijian was not a written language until Christian missionaries put spoken Fijian in writing. The missionaries used some English letters in unusual ways—for example, *c* sounds like *th, b* sounds like *mb,* and *q* sounds like *ng*! The name of 1800s Fijian leader Cakobau is pronounced "thak-OM-bau."

Work

About half of Fiji's workers earn their money at farming, forestry, or fishing. Sugarcane is the most important crop, and many people work growing the cane or processing it into sugar. Other important crops include coconut, rice, and coffee. The forests produce valuable hardwoods, and fish and other seafoods are harvested from the oceans. Some people work in mines digging out gold and copper.

Most people in towns work in businesses. Many provide services to **tourists** who visit the islands. Tourism has been Fiji's most important source of money next to sugar. Tourist attractions, hotels, and resorts all bring visitors and provide jobs. Tourists also buy island-made art such as baskets, carved wood items, and shell jewelry. The nation's recent unrest has made many tourists reluctant to visit.

©Jack Fields/CORBIS

A Man Carving A Wooden Head

©Jack Fields/CORBIS

Gold Miners Taking A Break

©Jack Fields/CORBIS

Suva

Villagers Fishing Together

A Man
And A Boy
Cooking
Over A
Hot Spring

Nandi

©Neil Rabinowitz/CORBIS

Foods in Fiji show influence from native Fijian culture as well as India, China, and Europe. Popular foods in Fijian cooking include fish, other seafoods, chicken, pork, beef, rice, yams, taro and cassava roots, and *lolo* (coconut milk). Tropical fruits and greens are also enjoyed.

Traditionally, Fijians steamed foods in an earth oven (*lovo*) filled with hot stones. They placed the food in the *lovo,* covered it with leaves, and then left it to cook. The traditional Fijian drink is *kava,* made from the shredded root of a pepper plant. Kava is used in many Fijian ceremonies.

A Man Making Kava

©Charles & Josette Lenars/CORBIS

A Woman Selling Produce At A Market In Nandi

© Ted Streshinsky/CORBIS

People who came to Fiji from other lands brought their cooking styles, too. Indians brought the traditional cooking methods of their native land. Spicy Indian curries are popular. Indian meals are usually served with soup (*dahl*) and rice or *roti,* a round, flat bread used to pick up food.

Musicians At A Kava Ceremony

©Jack Fields/CORBIS

Fiji's people have always enjoyed storytelling, singing and dancing, especially when celebrating special events. Musicians accompany singers and dancers on bamboo flutes, shell trumpets, panpipes, and drums. Water sports have also been popular, including swimming and diving. Today Fijians also enjoy soccer, cricket, and other sports—especially rugby.

Holidays include New Year's on January 1, National Youth Day in February, Constitution Day in July, and Fiji Day in early October. Christians celebrate Christmas and Easter, while Hindus celebrate *Diwali* (the "Festival of Lights"). Different towns and islands also have their own local festivals. Suva's week-long Hibiscus Festival in August features dancing and parades. The town of Nadi has a similar Bula Festival each July.

Rugby Players In A Scrum

©Jack Fields/CORBIS

Fiji's people are known for their friendliness and enjoyment of life. Perhaps someday you will be able to visit Fiji and enjoy its spectacular scenery and fascinating culture.

VANUA LEVU ISLAND

TAVEUNI ISLAND

KORO ISLAND

Nadi Lautoka

VITI LEVU ISLAND

Suva

KADUVU ISLAND

Children
Playing
Soccer On
Viti Levu

Area

About 7,100 square miles
(18,300 square kilometers)—about the size of New Jersey.
Of that, about 4,200 square miles are on the island of Viti Levu.

Population

About 790,000 people.

Capital City

Suva.

Other Important Towns

Lautoka, Nadi (pronounced NAHN-dee), Levuka.

Major Islands

Viti Levu, Vanua Levu, Taveuni, Kaduvu, Koro.

Flag

A light blue background with the cross of the British Union Jack in the upper left corner and
a shield to the right. The Union Jack stands for Fiji's long relationship with Great Britain.
The shield is from Fiji's coat of arms.

National Song

"The National Anthem of Fiji."

Currency

The Fiji dollar, which is divided into 100 cents.

Head of State

The president.

Head of Government

The prime minister.

Official Name

The Sovereign Democratic Republic of the Fiji Islands.

Water Lilies
In Bloom

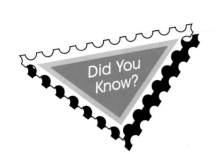

The whale's tooth, or tabua (pronounced "tam-boo-ah"), is a special item in traditional Fijian culture. For centuries Fijians have used whales' teeth in ceremonies, given them as gifts, and used them to show bonds between people or groups.

In traditional Fijian beliefs, spirits could give people the ability to walk on fire. Today, fire-walkers perform for tourists, walking across pits filled with white-hot stones. Some of Fiji's Indian Hindus also practice fire-walking for religious purposes.

Fiji is home to iguanas that came from Central or South America long ago. Scientists believe these early iguanas floated across the ocean on plant "rafts." Their thick skin protected them from the hot sun, and they got rid of ocean salt by sneezing it through their noses! Today, when one of Fiji's rare crested iguanas gets upset, its green color changes to black.

Animals and plants brought to Fiji by settlers have caused drastic changes in the islands' environment. Mongooses, for example, were brought from India to kill rats in Fiji's sugarcane fields. Instead, the mongooses became pests themselves, killing the islands' snakes and birds.

	FIJIAN	HOW TO SAY IT
Hello	ni sa bula	nee sah mBOO-lah
Good-bye	ni sa moce	nee sah MOR-they
Please	yalo vinaka	VEE-nah-kah
Thank You	vinaka	VEE-nah-kah
Yes	io	EE-oh
No	sega	SENG-ah
One	dua	nDOO-ah
Two	rua	ROO-ah

constitution (kon-stih-TOO-shun)
A constitution is a document that states how a nation's government will work. Fiji has changed its constitution in recent years.

continents (KON-tih-nents)
Continents are Earth's largest land masses and are surrounded mostly by water. Fiji's islands are far from any continent.

coup (KOO)
In politics, a coup is the sudden overthrow of a nation's government. The Fijian army took over the government in a 1987 coup.

dialect (DY-uh-lekt)
A dialect is a different form of a language spoken by people in a certain area. Indo-Fijians often speak a dialect of Hindi.

hostage (HOSS-tidj)
A hostage is someone who is kept prisoner until a demand is met. In 2000, rebels held some of Fiji's leaders hostage.

indentured servants (in-DEN-tchurd SER-vents)
An indentured servant is a person who signs an agreement to work for someone for a period of time. In the late 1800s, many Indians came to Fiji as indentured servants, promising to work on farms for 5 years.

inhabited (in-HAB-ih-ted)
A place is inhabited if someone lives there. Of Fiji's 332 islands, only 100 or so are inhabited, and the rest are uninhabited.

leeward (LEE-wurd)
Leeward means protected from or facing away from the wind. The leeward north and west sides of Fiji's islands are dryer.

parliament (PAR-leh-ment)
A parliament is a group of elected leaders who make a nation's laws. Fiji has a parliament.

thatched (THATCHT)
A thatched roof is made of layers of grass, reeds, or leaves. Traditional Fijian homes had thatched roofs.

tourists (TOOR-ists)
Tourists are visitors and vacationers from other countries. Some Fijians have jobs taking care of tourists.

tropical (TROP-ih-kull)
A place that is tropical has hot, moist weather year round. Fiji's climate is tropical.

windward (WIND-wurd)
Windward means facing into the wind. The windward south and east sides of Fiji's islands are wetter.

Index

Web Sites

Learn more about Fiji!

Visit our homepage for lots of links about Fiji:
http://www.childsworld.com/links.html

Note to Parents, Teachers, and Librarians:
We routinely verify our Web links to make sure they're safe, active sites—so encourage your readers to check them out!